Net
Entrepreneurs
Only

Net Entrepreneurs Only

Only

10 ENTREPRENEURS TELL THE STORIES OF THEIR SUCCESS

GREGORY K. ERICKSEN, ERNST & YOUNG LLP

John Wiley & Sons, Inc.

New York · Chichester · Weinheim · Brisbane · Singapore · Toronto

Published by John Wiley & Sons, Inc.
Published simultaneously in Canada.

No part of this publication may be reproduced, stored in a retrieval system or transmitted in any form or by any means, electronic, mechanical, photocopying, recording, scanning or otherwise, except as permitted under Sections 107 or 108 of the 1976 United States Copyright Act, without either the prior written permission of the Publisher, or authorization through payment of the appropriate per-copy fee to the Copyright Clearance Center, 222 Rosewood Drive, Danvers, MA 01923, (978) 750-8400, fax (978) 750-4744. Requests to the Publisher for permission should be addressed to the Permissions Department, John Wiley & Sons, Inc., 605 Third Avenue, New York, NY 10158-0012, (212) 850-6011, fax (212) 850-6008, E-Mail: PERMREQ@WILEY.COM.

This publication is designed to provide accurate and authoritative information in regard to the subject matter covered. It is sold with the understanding that the publisher is not engaged in rendering legal, accounting, or other professional services. If legal advice or other expert assistance is required, the services of a competent professional person should be sought.

ISBN: 0-471-38146-2

Printed in the United States of America.
10 9 8 7 6 5 4 3 2 1

CONTENTS

ACKNOWLEDGMENTS

This book, our third now in a series on entrepreneurs, gives new meaning to the word *collaboration* in terms of those to whom we owe our thanks. As always, we are most grateful to the 10 Net entrepreneurs profiled in these pages who gave us their time—when they have so little of it—and their stories—when so many clamor for them—with such personal thoughtfulness and insight into the New Economy that they are busily creating. And once again, Edward Wakin came through with his excellent research and reporting skills. Words of thanks fail me here, but luckily, they never fail Ed!

To those in the Ernst & Young family, a word of appreciation goes out to Andrea Mackiewicz, whose continued editorial and publishing capabilities make this series happen. The board members of the Entrepreneur Of The Year Institute provided direction and guidance, as did our EOY director, Nancy Clark. As always, my wife Gina is the biggest supporter of my work—as are my children, Alexander, Nicole, and Jonathan, who I am sure will emerge as leaders in the next generation of Net entrepreneurs. Thank you all.

Gregory K. Ericksen
Dallas, Texas

INTRODUCTION

Internet entrepreneurs have established themselves as leading players in the information age by seizing upon opportunities unprecedented in the history of business. Never before has there been such rapid access to financial success. Never before has the door been so wide open to entrepreneurship, to such sudden growth by new companies, and to such accumulation of wealth virtually overnight.

As a business environment, the Internet world calls for a personality portfolio that comes naturally to entrepreneurs. It demands a willingness to take risks, a wholehearted commitment to the enterprise, a sense of timing, and a readiness to act fast. The challenge of the Internet is not technology, which is the enabler. The challenges and the opportunities are based on problem solving and innovations that deliver value. Ideas that make a difference can and must be put into action quickly. No one's lunch is safe from the competition, not just in the long run but right now.

The networked age has shown itself to be exponentially

different from any past revolution in the speed, openness, and magnitude of opportunity. Tycoons of the past measured success in terms of decades. Now it's years, months, even days, depending on the date of a company's Initial Public Offering (IPO). In the four years between 1995 and mid-1999, the market capitalization of some 100 Internet companies that issued stock in 1995 surpassed $250 billion. The market value of U.S. companies with substantial Internet revenue exceeded $3 trillion. Twenty of the largest companies with significant Internet-based revenues have a combined market value of $2.4 trillion.

Take, for example, priceline.com (whose entrepreneur-founder is included in this book): Three months after going public the company went from a $16 stock price to $140, creating an $18.5 billion company. All of this was based on a simple but irresistible invitation to consumers—"name your own price"—with online trading.

The Internet Economy, as it is called, surpassed $300 billion in revenues in 1998, with the U.S. portion alone amounting to one of the top 20 economies in the world. In just five years since the introduction of the World Wide Web, the Internet Economy rivaled century-old sectors like energy ($223 billion), automobiles ($350 billion), and telecommunications ($270 billion). Also daunting is the average revenue per Internet Economy worker: $250,000 or about 65 percent higher than their counterparts in the Industrial Economy.[1]

Barron's has pointed out how the Internet "has evolved from a novelty into a dominant force in the IPO market" by citing what happened during the first half of 1999. Internet stocks represented more than 50 percent of IPOs during that period. A year earlier in the same period, it was only 7.5 percent and for 1997 a mere 5.5 percent.[2]

---

[1]"The Internet Economy Indicators," developed and compiled by the University of Texas at Austin, June 1999.
[2]*Barron's*, July 19, 1999, p. 21.

Commentators have been breathless in their attempts to describe the Internet phenomenon, pointing out that it is much more than networks, software, and computers, among many technologies. It's "a catalyst of change, a new mass medium, a culture, a mindwarp, new things never before imagined."[3] No company wants to be left behind, small companies included. The market research firm, IDC, based in Framingham, Massachusetts, has reported that the number of small businesses (under 100 employees) with web pages doubled in 1998 over the previous year and was in the process of nearly doubling again in 1999 to more than 2 million businesses. A Bank One report in mid-1999 found that about one out of five small businesses with 10 or fewer employees had web sites. The price of entry is low, as little as $300, and the monthly cost within easy reach of almost any business. More than one expert has warned that even small enterprises that stay out of the Internet are in danger of going out of business completely.[4]

Online entrepreneurs have led the way in what Bill Gates calls "a new way of life"—the Web lifestyle. The success stories in this book reveal how, when, where, and with what results these men and women have taken traditional entrepreneurship to new heights. As millennial successors to the entrepreneurs of the industrial age, they are leading companies into the Internet age. In talking about the high stakes, a Silicon Valley entrepreneur told the *New York Times* that "you weren't even a player in the Valley with less than $100 million."[5]

In discussing the "high-return, high-growth opportunities" of the Internet marketplace, the renowned Massa-

---

[3]J. Neil Weintraut in *Architects of the Web* by Robert H. Reid, New York: John Wiley & Sons, 1997, p. xiii.
[4]*USA Today*, August 3, 1999, p. B3.
[5]Po Bronson, "Instant Company," *New York Times Sunday Magazine*, July 11, 1999, p. 47.

chusetts Institute of Technology (MIT) economist Lester Thurow characterized the successful players: "Those who become economic winners understand the new technologies, are lucky enough to be in the right place at the right time and have the skills to take advantage of these new situations. They become very, very rich."[6]

Internet entrepreneurs have acted on what was not obvious when they took their chances on the way to storybook successes. In the beginning, even venture capitalists, the most adventurous of all financial players, either "didn't get it" or didn't believe what was happening. Internet entrepreneurs proceeded to transform the *what if* question that has characterized the creative process. The *what if* answers emerged in terms of the capabilities and functionality of the digital world and the connectivity of the Web.

The question has been changed to *how*—how to customize services, how to deliver pinpointed information, how to guide users through the avalanche of data to *exactly* what they want. A purification plant manager needs a pinch valve? The manager need only log onto a web site that lists all the suppliers in the industry and order the part immediately. Need to sell a centrifuge that spins chemical compounds at higher speeds than competing centrifuges? The U.S. firm in question closed a $1 million sale with an Australian factory of a European pharmaceutical company. The seller would never even have known the buyer existed if it weren't for a web site created by the entrepreneurs behind VerticalNet, Inc. (profiled in this book).

Online entrepreneurs have taken advantage of the Internet to apply a classical formula for starting a business: They identify a marketable offering. In the case of

---

[6]*Newsday* column, reprinted October 26, 1999, in *Daily Hampshire Gazette*, Northampton, MA.

the Internet, this means either doing something that couldn't be done before or doing what could be done but doing it faster, better, and cheaper. It could only happen on the Internet and it happened faster than with any previous technology for transmitting information.

Establishing 50 million users as a threshold for a mass medium, 1997 was a turning point for the Internet. Radio took 40 years to hit the 50-million threshold, TV 13 years, cable TV 10 years, the personal computer (PC) 16 years. It took the Internet 4 years. Estimated at 8 to 30 million in 1995 and 28 to 40 million in 1996, it surpassed 100 million by the end of 1997.[7] Entrepreneurs came along, saw, and conquered opportunities by identifying and acting on ways to reach and serve the global explosion of customers online. Customers, in turn, are responding to the changes in transactions—the process of buying and selling. Sellers no longer control information, much less pricing. Online entrepreneurs are putting information, selection, and pricing in the hands of the customer. Smiling salespeople who make friends with customers as a prelude to making a sale are being replaced by hot web sites where information does the talking. Paths to success are paved by online entrepreneurs who figure out what to deliver and then take advantage of the Internet *how.*

Nowhere has this entrepreneurial process found a more welcoming environment than in the United States and nowhere are the fields of enterprise more fertile. According to one estimate, 50 percent of the U.S. gross domestic product is primed for e-commerce. Meanwhile, venture capitalists have created a land of plenty for U.S. investors. In 1999, venture capitalists invested more than in the previous three years combined and over 65

---

[7]U.S. Department of Commerce, "The Emerging Digital Economy," 1999.

percent of 1999 venture capital went to Internet-related companies.[8]

But make no mistake, the addresses of online entrepreneurs are not geographic but global and their marketplace is the world. It can be argued that by its newness, openness, and availability, the online marketplace is made for entrepreneurs everywhere. It is their natural habitat. It provides soil and sunlight for ideas, enables them to grow their businesses rapidly, and provides a rich harvest in customers and capital. No entrepreneur could ask for a more enticing and conducive landscape in which to plant a business and reap its rewards.

Of the different ways to tell the story of the Internet phenomenon, none is more revealing than the stories of its entrepreneurs, enriched by their own recollections and reflections. It is also a revealing exploration of what it takes to be an entrepreneur who is making changes in a changing world, like an actor who's playing his or her part while also helping to write the play itself. They are the ultimate entrepreneurs. They saw opportunities, took the risks to exploit them, and succeeded to an unimaginable degree (even to them). Jerry Yang, cofounder of Yahoo!, the world's largest Internet portal, compares the newness of doing business on the Web to "being dropped off a helicopter, and you're the first guy skiing down the hill. You don't know where the tree is, you don't know where the cliff is, but it's a great feeling."

The online entrepreneurs in this book talk openly and personally about what was going on in their minds and how it feels skiing down the hill. They deal with the kinds of questions that everyone wants to ask them, and in their answers they explain what they are all about as well as the Internet. On one hand, they are like all other entrepreneurs—making better mousetraps. On the other,

---

[8]*Wall Street Journal,* February 7, 2000.

there has never been anything quite like the Internet. It hasn't changed the rules of profit and loss, but it has speeded up exponentially how fast things happen and how soon success is measured. Talk to them about what has happened to them and to their companies and how they think it all happened, and you will get answers to questions about being an entrepreneur in the online world that all of us now inhabit.

- How did they come up with the ideas for their successful enterprises?
- What are they like as entrepreneurs? What part did their background, education, training, and experience have in their success?
- What talents and skills counted the most?
- What have they learned? What advice can they offer?
- What differences have they made in their industries and marketplaces?
- How are they different from the competition and from the rest of us?
- How do they keep going?
- What can we learn from them about what it takes to be an entrepreneur? What is the difference between a "bricks" and a "clicks" entrepreneur?
- Where are the next opportunities in a networked world?

The entrepreneurs featured in this book have been singled out and vetted by Ernst & Young in the course of identifying recipients of the professional services firm's prestigious Entrepreneur of the Year Awards. Collectively, they are in the top tier of the who's who of the business revolution brought about by a networked world where dot-com can identify entrepreneurs who have become sudden billionaires.

JAY S. WALKER—PRICELINE.COM

"Name Your Own Price"

Jay S. Walker—Priceline.com

"Name Your Own Price"

When Jay S. Walker was a 13-year-old summer camper who visited the camp store with his friends to buy candy, they didn't see what he saw. They saw chocolate bars, Cracker Jacks, and cookies. He saw a marketing opportunity and a chance to set up an alternate channel for selling candy to his fellow campers. He proceeded to make a profit by buying in bulk and undercutting the prices at the camp store. With the grin of someone who enjoys coming up with winning sales propositions and who identifies himself as primarily a marketer, he recalls with relish being a teenage "black marketer" who was "serving" customers. "I simply bypassed the monopoly."

Thirty years later at age 43, he was the multibillionaire founder of priceline.com, the online phenomenon with the buyer-driven slogan, "Name Your Own Price." When *Barron's* inventoried the IPO centimillionaires who emerged in the 12 months preceding June 30, 1999, he topped the list. Among all of them, including the two-thirds whose fortunes were Internet based, Jay Walker was number one at $6.7 billion. (At one point in the world of high-flying Internet valuations, priceline.com's stock soared past 140 and Jay's 49 percent share topped $9.5 billion.)

In the 30 years between summer camp and priceline.com, Jay never stopped thinking of marketing ideas and putting them to work in 15 different enterprises that qualified as winning ideas even when they failed as businesses. "The hardest thing about being an entrepreneur," he says, "is knowing when to quit. It's an ego thing. Most entrepreneurs view quitting as a failure, when it's really the end of an inning, not the end of the game."

Appropriately, Jay's priceline.com success earned him the title of The Consummate Entrepreneur from a leading trade publication, *Target Marketing,* which named him the 1998 Direct Marketer of the Year. In an authoritative close-up of Jay, marketing expert Denny Hatch called him "a revolutionary whose vision and execution" of his vision "may put a stamp on commerce, communications and business well into the 22nd century."

When Jay talks about marketing, he means business.

I view myself as a marketer who solves problems using the mechanism of marketing. What marketers do—and it's widely misunderstood—is create business solutions that are end-to-end processes. I would say that I'm a marketer who invents business methods that are almost exclusively market driven. The problem always comes first. And, by the way, problems are not secret and they generally aren't that difficult to isolate. What's difficult today is to recognize that there are entirely new tools to solve the problems. In the past, because so many problems required physical solutions, you were highly constrained on what you could do. Now that so many solutions are in the information layer of the process, you can quickly deploy real solutions that are information solutions. Look at priceline with more than 2 million customers in 15 months. What you see is an information solution. We decoded a solution that was information.

With priceline.com, Jay pioneered a new type of e-commerce that meets the consumer demand for goods and services below the retail price line—hence the name of the company. Jay's solution turns the traditional auction formula upside down—changing the perspective from high bidder to low-priced sellers, shifting power from the seller with offerings in demand to buyers who want to pay less, and changing focus from items in rare supply to products and services in excess supply.

Jay's unique patented business model is a "demand collection" system that provides what have been called "take-it-or-leave-it" bids by consumers. It is unlike any of the five historic methods of buying and selling: barter, the open-air marketplace, retail (with prices fixed by the seller), auction (with many bidders for one item), and request for proposal (RFP) in which buyers openly solicit bids from many suppliers.

Add Jay's business model, possible only in the Internet world: Patent No. 5,794,207: "Method and apparatus for a cryptographically assisted commercial network system designed to facilitate buyer-driven conditional purchase offers." Or as graphically stated in a priceline.com document: What the system does is "literally hang buyer money on a 'clothesline' for sellers to see. Attached to the money is a note describing what the seller is agreeing to in order to take the money down off the clothesline."

Conditional purchase offers (CPOs) are at the heart of Jay's marketing invention. The Internet news magazine, the *Industry Standard,* called it "a whole new way of doing business on the Internet" after hearing him describe his thinking process. "When we invented CPOs, we were struggling to solve a problem. It was clear to us that dynamic pricing mechanisms had a role to play in all of the future of commerce. The problem was: Who needed dynamic pricing the most? Obviously, anybody with perishable or excess inventory needs to price dynamically in order to clear the market."

The process appeals to both companies and consumers while profiting the service provider, priceline.com, which collects fees and benefits from the "spread"—when buyers get what they want at a price higher than what the seller asks. For companies, it resolves a catch-22 problem. On one hand, they want to sell offerings that would otherwise be unsold or unused—plane seats, hotel rooms, mortgage funds, the latest car models. On the other hand, if companies publicly discount their retail prices or sell through a liquidator, they undercut their retail channels and alienate their full-price customers. Priceline.com enables sellers to meet customer demand anonymously without hurting themselves and their sales channels.

On the customer side, the process appeals to the many people who want to pay less and are flexible (but still selective) about what, when, and where—*what* brands they buy, *when* they want to take advantage of a service, *where* they make a purchase. They name their price and guarantee their bid with a credit card. Priceline.com circulates the customer's offering price to participating sellers who can then decide to sell or not. Since the customers don't know which brand they will get until after their offering price is accepted, retail channels are not disrupted and can continue to sell to customers who will pay a premium for a particular brand or specific product and service.

The seller has every right to refuse to sell, but it's the buyer who is establishing the offering price for the "billion-dollar-arm" (in this case, a high-end price, but the buyer is still setting the price). In effect, the same thing happened with airline tickets, the first offering from priceline.com when it began operations on April 6, 1998 (attracting more than a million customers in its first week). This was followed by hotel rooms the following October, then home mortgages and cars, followed by rental cars and groceries. The deal is an up-front exchange: Buyers surrender flexibility (but not quality) in exchange for a lower price; sellers get less than their standard price, but less is better than nothing.

Airline tickets provided a fast takeoff because of an "inventory" problem for major airlines. Each day they took off with an average of 500,000 empty seats—revenue lost, never to be recovered. Priceline.com enables customers to make a reasonable offer under set conditions covering advance booking, departure times, and nonrefundable, nontransferable tickets. Jay met the challenge of getting the word out on what he offered by relying largely on the old-fashioned medium of radio, featuring *Star Trek*'s William Shatner as spokesperson. In 150 days with a modest $25 million outlay for a major advertising campaign, priceline.com became the second-most-recognized Internet brand in the country among adults, second only to Amazon.com.

Priceline.com sold 300,000 airline tickets in its first 12 months. When hotel rooms were added, 100,000 rooms were booked in the first 3 months. When home mortgages were offered, homeowners sought $1 billion in the first 3 months, with $125 million in financing approved. When the selling of new cars was tested in the New York area, $11 million in sales was generated within 9 months. In priceline.com's fast start, new customers rushed in at the rate of 5,900 a day and in no time at all they let it be known that they wanted more offerings. Surveys showed that customers wanted the site to add computers, TVs, camcorders, stereos, car insurance, cable TV service, credit card interest rates, cruises, rental cars, and long-distance telephone service.

With priceline.com, Jay is doing what he has always done as entrepreneur/marketer: Identify problems and find solutions that can make money. That's how you know the solutions are worth anything. In college, he set out to market a solution to winning at Monopoly after becoming the northeast champion and a recognized player of world-champion caliber (who was banned from competition because of his winning ways). His strategy worked regardless of the uncertainties of the dice. When Jay approached Parker Brothers with the offer to write a book about winning at Monopoly, he got an answer he never forgets: "If you do, we will sue you!" He published the book anyway on his own—and it became a success that failed. The book, *1000 Ways to Win Monopoly Games,* sold more than 100,000 copies and earned $50,000 in profits. Parker Brothers sued, as threatened, and though it later dropped the suit, Jay's legal fees devoured his profits.

His next venture in college was another winner that lost. He dropped out in his junior year to start a weekly newspaper that went head-to-head with the local *Ithaca Gannett Daily.* He even obtained a $500,000 loan from Bankers Trust to finance a paper run by a college dropout and a staff of college students. This time, as he recalls, he "ticked off Gannett big time." The newspaper chain sent in a SWAT team to launch a competitive weekly that gave away most of its advertising. In five months, Jay's *Midweek Observer* went out of business and he went back to school for a B.S. degree in industrial relations from Cornell University.

As the son of a successful real estate developer, Jay had a firsthand role model in entrepreneuring. His father thought that, after his son's Monopoly experience, real estate was where he should head. To his mother, a champion bridge player, Jay ascribes the sense of competitiveness he developed while growing up in Queens, New York. Both parents encouraged his penchant for risk taking. For Jay Walker, there was no question. Entrepreneuring was his career through success and setbacks, ideas that worked and those that didn't. The following postgraduation ventures deserved a better fate.

• *Visual Technologies:* a company that manufactured light sculptures and sold them by catalogs. One thousand copies of the $1,200 sculptures sold out in just 30 days, but Jay's manufacturing facility couldn't keep up with the demand. The business failed.

• *Advertising in catalogs:* an idea born out of Jay's success in selling light sculptures via catalogs. He came up with a plan for selling ads in catalogs to major companies, signing up 12 immediately. Jay remembers the venture as a "leveraged business method" in which he didn't touch the underlying business or inventory. He just sold ads as he would for a magazine—without any editorial, production, or circulation costs. It was an appealing idea that foundered on a problem. In practice, catalogers wouldn't commit to setting aside space where and when the ads would have the greatest impact. Ads would be postponed to later editions of catalogs or to the back of the book. What Jay describes in recollection as a "marriage of two unwilling partners" lost money and folded.

• *Selling catalogs:* to consumers in bookstores and newsstands so that they could get the catalogs they wanted immediately. Jay set up the process based on "a negative cost of goods." The catalogs didn't cost him anything. The customers paid $2 for catalogs of choice with the price offset by a $5 discount sticker. The retailer kept an enticing 60 percent of the catalog price. The companies happily picked up new customers. It was an immediate success that was derailed by the cover stickers, for postal codes and for the discount, on the catalogs. They fell off because the printer used the wrong glue. "The business was profitable from day one," Jay reports—then the stickers fell off en route to the retailer and the business collapsed.

Then there were the Jay Walker successes that succeeded all the way to the bottom line and beyond. He sold Federal Express on providing overnight or second-day delivery for catalog companies, generating millions in additional revenue for FedEx. It was a natural winner, enabling customers to get fast delivery throughout the year and Christmastime retailers to sell goods right up to a couple of days before the shopping rush ended. He teamed up with Chuck Tannen, a leading figure in the magazine industry, to set up the Direct Marketing to Business Conference, which was eventually sold for a multi-million-dollar price. Next, he and Tannen launched a successful trade magazine for direct marketing organizations. In another partnership enterprise, Walker identified a problem in the magazine industry—annual renewals: "No other service in the world forces its customers to reevaluate its usefulness once a year and decided whether or not to continue." The highly profitable solution is automatic renewal tied to a credit card until and unless the subscriber cancels. It became New-Sub Services, whose profits in the millions enabled Jay to set up Walker Digital, his own think tank. It has one ongoing goal: to come up with new solutions for business methods and patent them. Its first soaring success is priceline.com, which uses 19 of Walker Digital's patents.

Reviewing his successes and his failures, Jay speaks as a current billionaire who has "had a negative net worth for most of my life." He has gone completely broke four times so he speaks from firsthand experience when he compares the winners and losers and then identifies the reasons why—almost.

> *Generally when you fail you know why and generally when you succeed you're much less sure. Failure, like death, has very specific causes. I didn't capitalize right, I didn't understand the market properly, I didn't understand my customers and competition properly. As a result, I failed. You can almost always put your finger on a failure. Success is far more complex. Success is about the interrelationship of a wide number of factors. I use the term a garden as a metaphor. A successful garden isn't about one thing or two things. It's about a whole garden. It's how it works together. It's the whole garden that's successful. An ecosystem is a good parallel. Great businesses are like great ecosystems. When you succeed, it's usually because you've figured out how to balance the 5 and 10 critical variables in a way that is sustainable for the whole. It's almost never about one thing. You see businesses that have enormous sales and fail and you see businesses with very little sales that succeed. You see businesses that have high profits at the start and fail. Success is not about one thing. That's why it's so elusive— because you have to do a lot of things right to succeed. Whereas you only have to do one big thing wrong to fail. That's business.*

In the online world, as Jay points out, there's a transforming new dimension to problem solving and the pursuit of success.

> *We look at solutions on the Net in two groups: There are transported forms and there are indigenous forms. A transported form is something that exists in the real world and that gets transported on the Net. I've got a*

catalog in print, I'll put a catalog on the Net. An indigenous form is one that can only exist on the Net. There can be 50,000 different prices on the Net all at the exact same moment in time and each customer can name his or her own price and each seller can decide in that moment in time whether to accept that price. This could never exist in a bricks-and-mortar context.

As to problems, there are no secrets. Maxwell House has to figure out how it's going to sell more coffee. Wal-Mart has to figure out how it's going to keep customers from going to Kmart. American Airlines has to figure out how it's going to get more people on planes. You name it, the problems generally aren't that difficult to isolate. What's difficult is to recognize that there are entirely new tools to solve the problems. In the past, because so many problems required physical solutions, you were highly constrained on what you could do. Now that so many solutions are in the information layer of the process, you can quickly deploy real solutions that are information solutions. I mean look at priceline with more than 2 million customers in 15 months. What you see is an information solution.

As to using technology, it's not a magic box. It's still a computer at the end of the day. You can hire programmers to execute what you want if you can describe what you want very specifically. If you ask technologists to invent your business, then you're going to have a business that doesn't work. But you can ask technologists to implement what you want the software to do. They are very available and they may be expensive, but not any more so than if you wanted to build a steel mill.

If online entrepreneurs are divided into those who figure out how to carry on established business practices faster and better on the Internet and those who invent new ways of doing business via the Internet, then it's obvious where Jay Walker belongs and why the *Industry Standard* selected him in 1999 as the "person with the most original ideas for Net businesses." Priceline.com personifies Jay's own description of the quintessential online entrepreneur: "What very few people have done is start with the Internet and build a derivative business. Priceline is a business that was built by starting with the Internet and saying 'What is the Internet good for?' "

Idea-focused, invention-centered, patent-directed Jay is interested in launching ideas rather than companies. "Starting companies is very hard and time-consuming," he says. "You want to keep those to a minimum." Instead, he's interested in licensing patents to established companies. When *Forbes* magazine asked him to look into the future, the quintessential Jay Walker emerged, someone who's always trying to think ahead of the rest of the business world and definitely ahead of where he is now. He sounds like a coach planning for the next season or, more appropriately, like a mathematician at the blackboard mapping an equation from here to infinity.

> *Computing is becoming universal. Mips [millions of instructions per second of processing power] will be free and ubiquitous. Mips trend to zero [cost] and bandwidth trends to infinity. Network access trends to continuous. What we do at Walker Digital is ask,* How will business be reinvented, given that reality? *It's a question most businesses are not working on.*

Walker identifies the difference between the world of entrepreneurs before the Internet and after, reflecting on the fact that he succeeds by capitalizing on the difference.

> *There is a fundamental difference between an entrepreneur on the Internet and an entrepreneur off the*

Internet. In the bricks-and-mortar world—whether it's an auto parts firm, a retail shop, a chain store, or a computer manufacturer—physicality imposes an enormous amount of restraints that you've got to deal with. For information-based entrepreneurs, nonphysicality means a completely different reality and a completely different set of tools to deal with. For example, a physical entrepreneur cannot scale from zero to 5 million of anything in a matter of a month. The newest version of Netscape could be on 6 million desktops in an hour. Amazon can do something and in one minute have 100,000 new customers. It's as if QVC, which was a dramatically successful launch, were suddenly the rules of all the games—without having to go sign up cable systems. Even QVC had to set up all these cable systems and build studios and build warehouses, etc. Net entrepreneurs are in a completely different place.

The great victory of our age is the victory of imagination over current belief. We, as a culture, have embraced the Star Trek *ethos—that if you can imagine it and it has a technological base to it, it's probably going to happen. Electrification would be the closest metaphor I can think of. Before there was electricity in everything, all prophecies left out electrification. Electrification changed everything when it became a practical tool for all of society, affecting every factory, every business, every government process, every military process, every household. Now, in the information age, the information architecture changes everything. The closest thing would be DNA, which is an information architecture. There is information coded in your DNA that makes you different from a tree. Interestingly, you share about 98 percent of your DNA in common with a tree—98 percent—and yet you don't think of a tree as being another form of information. You may think of a tree as being another species, but it's not. It's just different encoding of the same information.*

So what does Jay do? He never stops looking for ideas that "can be structured in a way that they effectuate significant change." His focus is not on ideas for their own sake, but ideas that can be put to work. He counts himself among idea-driven entrepreneurs, individuals who change, even create, an industry where one didn't exist before—the way Federal Express changed the system of delivery. Jay is at his best when he sits down with one of his teams at Walker Digital, "which work to create solutions to business problems."

Jay calls Walker Digital "a new way to think about the Internet and about the tools and powers of the Internet." It's modeled after Thomas Edison's famous laboratory in Menlo Park, New Jersey, in which teams, rather than solitary inventors, came up with discoveries. Jay regards that team approach, rather than the lightbulb, as Edison's greatest achievement. Something else that ties Jay's laboratory to Menlo Park is the practical focus. "When you study it, you find that Edison was a brilliant marketer. He never invented without a customer in mind and he would disdain any invention that wasn't practical in a commercially obvious way."

That's what happens at Walker Digital with its mixed staff of inventors and patent attorneys. The inventors invent. The lawyers protect their inventions with patents. The heart of the operation is "invention sessions" where Walker presents business problems in such areas as retailing, telecommunications, credit cards, lotteries, television, and vending machines. Teams take up the search for solutions under the personal direction of Walker, using the make-or-break test of commercial viability. Ideas and solutions that fail that test never make it to the patent attorneys.

The people around the table at Walker Digital sessions are carefully recruited by Jay; practically all of them are in their twenties or early thirties. They have all kinds of backgrounds—patent attorney, apprentice pastry chef, financial analyst, fine arts salesperson, management consultant, cryptography consultant, advertising intern, patent attorney, bus driver. They have degrees in law, business, applied economics, biology, philosophy, liberal arts, music, computer engineering. Not a parade of Ph.D.'s absorbed in their specialties, but rather a variety of B.A.'s mixed with law, business, and master's degrees. Walker describes it as his "own personal laboratory that works alongside an operating company [priceline.com] with very different cultures in how they address and solve problems, yet they work cooperatively."

> *In the people at Walker Lab, I look for overwhelming intellectual curiosity, for an ability to communicate, for a demonstrated capacity to think creatively. Also a good attitude about working in groups, a strong need to succeed, and an incredible desire for truth. On my part, I am one of those marketers that sit in the room analyzing and critiquing various solutions put forth by invention teams to solve very specific problems. So right now—when we finish talking—I'm going back to work on a set of problems that about 15 of us are working on. I'm going to spend the day [a Saturday] working on them. We're going to find a solution to that problem and when we do, it's going to look like an "aha." But it's not, it's going to be the result of a lot of hard work. Walker Digital is much more like a genetics laboratory than it is like anything else. In a genetics lab you're working hard to look for ways to structure the DNA to solve problems. It's no accident when you find it. You might be lucky in one sense of the word, but most of the time you're just disciplined. You're*

spending your time evaluating what might work and what might not.

The problem always comes first. I'm always thinking about ideas and problems. You can't find something you're not looking for. People who complain that they don't have enough ideas or that other people seem to have more ideas often don't realize that you need to be looking for ideas to find them. I spend most of my time looking, prospecting for ideas. I surround myself with people who are challenging and who themselves are looking for ideas. The vast majority of my time is spent in problem-solving sessions and meetings that are focused on finding the diamonds in the rough. I might be better at it because I've been working at problem solving for 25 years, but I don't believe there's any magic to it.

I read a lot—two to three hours a day, usually from 7 to 10 in the evening—and I use my reading time as sort of my private thinking time. I read a fair amount of physics—quantum mechanics. I read Kevin Kelly's book, Out of Control, *which I thought was a phenomenal book. I read books on biology. I have dozens of things that I read. I read hundreds of magazines a month on almost every subject. I read fast. I skim for what I'm interested in, but once I read I concentrate. I read the* Economist *and I read the* National Enquirer. *I don't think many people read both. I read anything that I find can stimulate my thinking about what people are doing and working on. All the time, I'm constantly ripping things out and writing notes.*

To manage priceline.com, he turned over daily operations to a major figure in the banking business, Richard Braddock, who was president of Citicorp when he resigned in 1992. Months later—after meeting and being impressed by Jay—he surprised Internet skeptics and stunned the investment community by signing on as chair and CEO of five-month-old priceline.com. Braddock had identified the Internet as "the ultimate leverage point" on the way toward targeted marketing. The same *Barron's* centimillionaire inventory that put Jay at the top of its list confirmed that Braddock knew what he was doing. *Barron's* listed him as number five at $2.1 billion.

Braddock has a firsthand insight into why Jay Walker has succeeded. He has the "impressive trait" of thinking "outside the box" and of coming up with ideas with a wide reach. "There are a lot of people around who have a good idea that they are peddling at some time or another. But there aren't many people like Jay, who have taught themselves to think in such a way that they actually come up with a string of great ideas that aren't even particularly segment- or niche-specific." Chuck Tannen, Jay's partner in his magazine ventures, goes further in depicting him: "Jay doesn't think out of the box; he thinks out of the planet."

The teenage camper who saw opportunity where others only saw candy bars still is a nonstop lookout scouting for what others miss, constantly analyzing the world around business, and test piloting ideas to see whether they fly and how high and fast. His natural habitat is Walker Digital, which already has generated more than 250 patent applications. More and more, he's leaving priceline.com in the hands of seasoned executives who know how to mind the store.

> I've hired and brought into priceline a senior management team that's really capable of handling a company that reached hundreds of millions of dollars in sales in its second year. You've got an entire senior management team that is used to handling companies and structures with hundreds of thousands and millions of customers. It's a management team that's

designed to take priceline through the next level with the necessary infrastructure and processes. You wouldn't ask entrepreneurs to do that. I am not a business executive in that sense. You wouldn't want to hire me to do that. Ultimately, my plan is to do what I do best—spending most of my time at Walker Digital. It's the laboratory that is inventing the business methods and models out of which will come businesses that create value. We own a set of ideas about the way commerce is done. Those ideas are unique, novel, different, and original; and we have invested in them and taught them to the world in the form of patents.

As to priceline.com, Jay looks ahead to its "long-term legacy." That depends, he says on "whether we can successfully introduce the first new pricing system in probably 500 years." It would fulfill the official prediction of priceline.com: "Someday, you'll buy everything this way." Meanwhile, he will do what he has always done, in bankruptcy or boom: "I've always been an entrepreneur. I start businesses for a living. I always have two or three businesses on the burner—like a farmer rotating crops."

His shift from being an entrepreneur in the bricks-and-mortar world to the online world was both natural and inevitable—because he is an entrepreneur. If fish are characterized as the last to realize that they're swimming in water, the smartest fish are the first to recognize the changes in the waters. Entrepreneurs go where the newer, bigger, and better opportunities are. Walker views entrepreneuring as a form of exploring.

In every age, there are great innovations toward which people who are explorers naturally move. When Columbus came along in the fifteenth century and said there's a whole new world out there, explorers would say, "Let's go check it out." That's the way it is with entrepreneurs. Primarily, they're opportunistically driven. They take ideas, assemble resources around the ideas, and take reasonable risks to bring those ideas into reality. As the Internet becomes the landscape—the most exciting landscape of our generation—it's natural that entrepreneurs migrate to that landscape. It's our new world.

MIKE MCNULTY & MIKE HAGAN— VERTICALNET

"We Get Qualified Eyeballs to Come to Very Focused Sites"

Left, *Mike McNulty;* right, *Mike Hagan.*

2

Mike McNulty & Mike Hagan— VerticalNet

"We Get Qualified Eyeballs to Come to Very Focused Sites"

One Sunday afternoon early in 1995 while visiting in-laws, Mike McNulty gave in—reluctantly—to his father-in-law's booster talk about something called the Internet. As a college student who had "run" from computer courses, he found his father-in-law's repeated rave notices about the information highway almost as interesting as a report on soybean futures. It was not for him. He was doing very well, thank you, as sales manager for *WaterWorld* magazine, selling ads the old-fashioned way for a successful trade publication, and that was that.

Then politeness transformed his career.

> *For more than a year, my father-in-law, who was a techie for Unisys, was talking repeatedly about surfing the Web. Finally, one Sunday when we were at his house, I said, "Okay, show me this Internet." He went to the Microsoft site in order to demonstrate on a really well-done web site and showed me that you could bounce from one company to another and once you got there you could access tons of information. He could*

go click and even send them an e-mail message. It seemed to me that for trade magazines this could provide a "bingo card" that works in real time—compared with checking off items on a list of companies in a printed form. Even though advertisers put weight on the number of responses to bingo cards, they couldn't get sales reps to follow up on them because anyone serious about buying isn't doing a product search by circling bingo cards in a magazine.

The value to the people I'd been selling ads to was so obvious. I couldn't see how it couldn't work. It wasn't limited to someone's name, address, and phone number. An engineer who needed a particular product could access virtually unlimited specific information, as much as the company wanted to give him. At the same time, he could go click and send the company a message that says, "I need this size for this application. This is how many I need and when I need them by." The key persons for my trade advertisers to reach were engineers, who back in '95 were already on the Internet. Here was a way to pull together all the information that engineers needed to do their job. If we could foster this kind of communication, it would be hugely valuable to companies that spend hundreds of thousands, even millions, of dollars in trade advertising. The much greater value of such communication was so obvious compared with what industrial companies got with trade advertising. It went way beyond what was available in magazines.

That first Internet experience was the origin of VerticalNet.

By Labor Day of that year, McNulty had launched VerticalNet in Horsham, Pennsylvania, near Philadelphia, with former college roommate Mike Hagan—and by Christmas they were on the verge of bankruptcy.

They confronted a classic entrepreneur's hurdle: too little financing. They had no doubt about the viability of their venture to establish web sites as online equivalents of advertisement-filled trade magazines. But they were early movers and the revenues didn't come in fast enough for their shoestring operation. McNulty had reached the point where his curriculum vitae was revised and ready to make the rounds, with selling insurance at the top of the list.

Then came a last-minute reprieve right out of the entrepreneur's play book. Four savvy (and tough-minded) investors each wrote personal checks for $25,000 to tide McNulty and Hagan over their immediate financial crisis. Four years later, after a major infusion of $16 million from a venture capital firm and an IPO, the emergency transfusion of $100,000 was worth $400 million as a 25 percent share of VerticalNet.

Another shoestring-to-riches Internet story, you might say, like winning the lottery. Not really. Of course, timing and being a first mover were crucial, but there's much more to this success story. The plot is woven out of friendship and mutual trust, commitment to an idea, marketplace savvy, risk taking, and overwhelming dedication to work. People close to the VerticalNet phenomenon add: "It couldn't have happened to two nicer guys."

"Two parts came together," Mike McNulty says. "I had the concept, saw the idea (online trade magazines) and its value, but I give Mike [Hagan] full credit for turning it into a business."

Hagan and McNulty (called "Hags" and "Nults" at the office) were friends going back to their days as roommates at St. Joseph's University in Philadelphia. For the decade after graduation in 1985, they stayed in touch, partied together, were groomsmen in each other's weddings. But go into business together? No one, particularly the two of them, would ever have predicted it. In fact, McNulty's wife wasn't surprised when he announced that he wanted to start a business of his own. But she was "shocked" about his business partner.

> *I think my wife's biggest shock was when I said that I was going into business with Mike Hagan. While Mike and I had always been great friends and stayed in touch, my wife's impression was that almost every time Mike and I got together, somehow it seemed to revolve around beer drinking in one way or another. The partnership hit her as coming out of left field. She was wholeheartedly supportive about my going into business, but wondered about going into business with my old pal. As to my job, she sensed that I was getting bored and frustrated. I had been selling ad space for 10 years since I got out of college and it was no longer a jump-out-of-bed-every-morning kind of a thing. She knew that I had been noodling around the idea of going into business and talking about it. Actually, Hagan was one of the people I was using as a sounding board. At one point, when we were talking about my idea, he took the bull by the horns and said, "I think you and I should do this." Why, I wondered, would he want to do this? He was in a tremendous position with Merrill Lynch, he had risen through the ranks to vice president and was reporting directly to a CFO of Merrill Lynch. I could see why I wanted to do this, but I didn't see why he did.*

Each saw the other as the risk taker. Hagan saw McNulty, with two children, a pregnant wife, and a big mortgage, walking away from a well-paid, secure position as sales manager for a successful trade magazine, where he had built a reputation and a following in the industry. McNulty saw Hagan walking away from a fast-track position at Merrill Lynch into a field where he was a stranger. Hagan had never even read a trade magazine.

But Hagan's eyes were wide open. For starters, he was impressed by McNulty's "infectious enthusiasm and energy." He figured that McNulty "as a smart guy" with family responsibilities wasn't going to chase a mirage. Also, as Hagan talked about the idea to technologists working on a Merrill Lynch project he was directing, it was making "a tremendous amount of sense." To a newly married 32-year-old whose wife also had a good-paying job at Merrill Lynch and who hadn't started a family yet, if ever it was time to try an entrepreneurial venture this was it."

Hagan recognized an entrepreneurial streak in himself. "I like taking risks. I don't like the status quo. I didn't envision the kind of success we have today, but I did think that this would be an exciting departure from the white-shirt, blue-tie, dark-suit culture of Merrill Lynch. I liked the chance to make a difference, to make a decision today and see the impact tomorrow, rather than at Merrill Lynch, which is very bureaucratic and has many layers of management. This would be an opportunity to go out there and be an entrepreneur."

As to McNulty's idea, Hagan foresaw that "business-to-business communication could ultimately be enhanced with the Internet as the platform." Projections by the respected Forrester Research have shown how right he was. By 2003, business-to-business commerce is expected to generate $1.3 trillion in revenues—12 times what Forrester projects for the consumer market. In VerticalNet, Hagan and McNulty set out to establish "vertical portals" that focus on a particular industry and its companies, players, products, and latest information. It's full-press narrow casting or as Hagan says: "We get qualified eyeballs to come to very focused sites."

Take, for example, VerticalNet's Water Online web site on the day the Editor's Choice was a portable turbidity

meter, air operated valves, and emergency release model-
ing software. The Deal of the Day was a "Chiller, 170 ton
@ 40 deg F; York Code-pak liquid chiller system. Package
Mdl #YSCACAS-1CGB; blt 1994. Has York ISN Code-pak
digital control center. Single rotary screw compressor Mdl
#163L; SN XLCM-460470. Driven by 170 HP; 3/60/460
volt; 3600 rpm drip-proof." For all but specialists, this
technology-saturated item makes as much sense as an
encrypted CIA message marked Top Secret. But to anyone in need of the Chiller, it's like offering a Mickey Man-
tle card to a collector of baseball memorabilia.

By the end of 1999, VerticalNet had some 50 different
sites, each hitting a carefully targeted business community in a specific part of a particular industry: advanced
technologies, communications, environmental, food and
packaging, food service/hospitality, healthcare/science,
manufacturing and metals, process, and service. Each
time McNulty and Hagan sought a new editor for a web
site in one of these industries, they recruited editors from
established trade publications, well informed about a
particular industry and well known by the people in it.
That provided instant credibility for a web site.

In going from 1 to 50 web sites, the problem from the
start was not the idea behind the enterprise, but the
money to keep it going. McNulty and Hagan came as close
as any committed entrepreneurs can come to bankruptcy. They started at full personal risk with $210,000
and four people—McNulty and Hagan (who, for all practical purposes, didn't draw a salary), Hagan's sister-in-law
(who went for months without getting paid), and a trade
editor (hired away to run their first web site, Water
Online). In starting off, web site production was done "on
the cheap," any spending devoted to sales and marketing
and to some advertising.

McNulty and Hagan, who quit their jobs, both tapped
every source of funds within reach. Hagan borrowed from

every relative and friend he could. McNulty used his house as collateral for a $50,000 loan from the U.S. Small Business Administration. Both soon borrowed on their credit cards to the maximum. While their first web site was attracting a high percentage of the potential audience in the area of water waste, they needed to expand to other sites and build revenues. Hagan's recollection is a quintessential entrepreneur's experience in which reality confronts the vision.

> *In 1995, we had the same attitude that any entrepreneur has had in uncharted waters. You're excited and you're concerned as well. It could evaporate. You could be dead wrong in your vision. I think that in the last couple of years everyone has sort of looked at what's going on in the Internet and said, "I want a piece of the action." They have illusions of grandeur and if they don't hit a home run or grand slam in the first year, they're awfully shocked because they just think that it's easy and anyone can do it. But it's much more difficult than most people think. You need a lot of hard work, a lot of luck, and a lot of good timing. We definitely did a lot of hard work, an enormous amount of hard work. I've given up my life for years. I've worked seven days a week, 16- to 18-hour days. Many is the night I've worked through to the morning. I used to play a lot of golf. I can say that I'd rather be here than play golf. We've also had good fortune—and in our moments of greatest despair we generally pulled a rabbit out of a hat.*

In particular, Hagan recalls the "darkest moment" when "$100,000 felt like a $100 million today." It was the December after they started and it was the kind of critical impasse that tests an entrepreneur's vision. They were running out of money when a chance conversation at a wedding reception led from one thing to another—to a quick transfusion of cash and an unforgettable last-minute reprieve. At the reception following the marriage of Hagan's younger brother on the day before New Year's Eve, Mike struck up a conversation with the chair of a real estate company that had received capital funding from an investment company. The realtor thought VerticalNet would interest the company and offered to establish contact.

Within a week, McNulty and Hagan were sitting opposite executives from the investment company. "What came through in the meeting," Hagan recalls, "was a little bit of desperation and certainly a lot of energy. Sometimes there's a fine line between the two. We described the same business plan we have today, all the elements of a virtual trade publishing company—editorial material, advertising, product directories, product showcase, a template we would replicate for many different industries." The reaction was positive, but they were left hanging and uncertain.

They were invited back the following week to meet more executives. McNulty and Hagan got the impression that their listeners were seriously considering a yes answer, but not then and there. They would get back to them by phone. More nail-biting. Hagan still remembers the redeeming phone call "like it was yesterday." Here was the deal: The investors valued VerticalNet at $400,000; four investors would put up one-fourth of the company valuation, each writing a check for $25,000. McNulty and Hagan grabbed the financial lifesaver and threw themselves into the business of staying in business.

They got to know each other better than ever and to appreciate each other more than ever. Working closely with Hagan, McNulty was impressed with how "smart" Hagan is and how flexible. "On paper, he was going to bring finance and accounting and I was going to bring

sales and marketing. It soon became obvious that everyone was going to have to sell and he was as good as any."
McNulty calls Hagan a "workhorse. . . . he has the ability
to work 80 hours a week. Literally, he's still here every
weekend." Hagan describes McNulty as "everyone's best
friend, the life of the party, but in the work environment,
he's absolutely driven." Then he adds: "Each one of us
would say that he trusts the other like a brother."

Their first portal, Water Online, an Internet version of
the magazine that McNulty worked for, was an online
trade journal for waste water. A flashback highlights how
far the Internet has come in so few years. Back "then"—
in 1995—McNulty was "running around the country"
demonstrating a web site in action (echoes of his first
Internet lesson). Some CEOs were still dismissing the
Web as the home of pornography. McNulty had to start
from scratch: "I used to begin an awful lot of demonstra-
tions by explaining that where the little arrow turns into
a finger it means that you can click and get more information. You had to take them from there to signing on the
dotted line." In the beginning, when companies signed up
for a $6,000 year-long contract to have a VerticalNet
"storefront" where they could describe and promote sales
of their products, it was a bet on McNulty, whom they
knew and respected. They were not entirely convinced,
nor clear about what they were buying into.

In the beginning, VerticalNet added sites by focusing on
businesses where engineers dominated the audience.
They were early users of the Internet and they needed the
same basic features in a web site: new product information, a directory of companies and products, up-to-date
industry information. And VerticalNet had a template
where the kinks were ironed out and it was ready to handle a technology-focused audience. "Engineers," as
McNulty knew from his experience in sales calls, "lived on
their computers all day." Sites aimed at property and

casualty insurance, dentists, and nurses would come in the later phases of expansion.

As with any trade publication, the revenue comes from advertising, but with the chance for customer contact that no print publication can match—a manufacturer's dream selling proposition. On the spot via the Internet. Here and now. Companies have the option of placing ads or setting up a storefront so that customers can contact them directly to make purchases. For the salesman in McNulty, it is an ultimate selling opportunity.

> *About 90 percent of our revenue is still advertising in nature. What we offer in our web sites is the connection, the ability to either link out to a company's web site or to generate sales by e-mail, with a direct lead to the company. Companies can buy extra banner ads to raise their visibility within our community. That's part of our model. Now we're adding the ability of a company to have a product release with a "buy me now" button for a direct transaction.*
>
> *From the start, our main inroad was to get value out of the Internet for industrial companies. Our mission has been to gather up people already on the Internet and enable them to communicate directly with a manufacturer for actionable, highly valuable sales leads. That's what we did, almost from day one. We set out to provide as complete a resource as possible for engineers whether their companies advertised with us or not. We wanted them to send us their technical articles and product releases, anything they would send to a magazine. As long as our web site editor feels it's good information for our audience, we'll publish it in an organized fashion. We'll promote the site so that the people you care about can read the information, including the name, address, and phone number of the company. We wouldn't charge them for that. We'd*

charge for connectivity, for the e-mail link to the company. It's an advertising model that's still our main source of revenue.

Hagan describes the stealthlike way they treaded into the marketplace. What was obvious to them still had not really registered with the thousands of trade publications around the country, who were not ready to take the plunge.

For the first few years, we tried to remain a stealth company as we rolled out our first 15 web sites. We didn't want to call attention to ourselves by the big guys. They knew that we were out there, but we didn't want to bring more attention to our company and our business model than we thought was necessary at the time. It was a business model that made a lot of sense and could be replicated in a lot of different industries that have a similar matrix and similar characteristics. So from the start we never had a bias toward one industry or were oriented toward one industry. Many people when they start a company only know one industry and so they look to dominate that one industry without developing a business model that could enjoy huge economies of scale by institutionalizing the model across several industries.

What we did first involved industries with an environmental focus, like pollution, solid waste, public works, power. Then we went into engineering-type manufacturing disciplines like pharmaceutical, chemical and food processing, and auto and gas. The first moves were to go after industries where the buyer or specifier is computer and modem enabled. After that, we looked at industries that were highly fragmented on both the vendor and buyer side.

We hired a consultant from almost day one. He's been driving a lot of the due diligence of these markets through a very methodical, disciplined approach with principles that we still use today. In developing new web sites, we look at spending from an advertising standpoint in trade journals. We also look at growth in trade show attendance. We look at a key data point— the growth of exhibitors at the major trade shows. We look at globality, how much is spent in the United States versus how much is spent globally. We love global industries. We look at whether these industries have a high rate of product innovation. Our consultant is out doing research six to eight months ahead of where we are today so we can make decisions on new sites. We also look at the competitive landscape in the industries we like in order to see if there's somebody out there that has market share on either the buy side or supply side where it makes sense to acquire them.

In tandem, McNulty and Hagan talk up the Internet world as a land of opportunity.

McNulty: *I can't imagine a more wide-open frontier to stake your claim [in] than the Internet. There's a ton of people in this business, but the opportunities are amazing. So I highly recommend it to anybody looking for opportunity. Take a look at what is going to be affected by the Internet. Learn about what is happening on the Internet, what's possible, what's coming down the pike. Then take a look at the industry you're in and how it's going to affect the business scale. Opportunities come from melding the real world with an understanding of what's coming. Look for the chance to stake out a territory.*

But I wouldn't get caught up in the technology. I think the success that our company has had has been

*largely because we recognized a value we could pro-
vide to a marketplace. Better sales leads was the original value. Then our job is to make the best use of
technology as it evolves to provide more value to our
audiences. We've always had a business approach,
not an Internet or technology approach, to what we do.*

Hagan: *We used to say that we're at the top of the
first inning, but maybe it's the top of the second
inning. It's still a long ball game, a time where you just
have to keep your head down and focus on what you
know works. The worst thing you can say about an
Internet company is that it makes slow mistakes. You
need to react quickly to the mistakes and not make
them again. Learn from them. You always want to
operate at turbo speed.*

To run the company beyond the first innings, McNulty
and Hagan weren't going to make the entrepreneur's mistake of trying to do it all themselves. They also decided
that the place to shop for the managing leadership they
wanted was not in the world of bricks and mortar, not if
they wanted to operate at turbo speed. Internet management called for Internet business experience. So they
recruited Mark Walsh, a Harvard M.B.A. who was a senior
vice president at America Online (AOL) and founder of its
business-to-business division. Before that, he had extensive online experience. ("I'm wired differently from my
classmates who got out of Harvard Business in 1980.")
McNulty provides an inside look at the down-to-earth,
practical process of hiring Walsh as president/CEO.

*We were going into our second round of institutional
financing, and we agreed with the rest of the board
that to take the company to the next level we could
use a higher profile guy who'd been around the block.*

We all agreed that if we could find the right CEO we could move the company to the next level, and I think that's exactly what happened. Mike and I met with Mark and we hit it off on a personal level. He knew that business-to-business communities were going to emerge and he saw the opportunity to jump to a company that had a head start. At the time, we had about ten verticals on board. So he jumped, and it's worked out tremendously.

Walsh, an outgoing former TV anchor who's a natural fit for the down-to-earth style of McNulty and Hagan, provided the trade magazine, *Folio,* with a colorful explanation of why traditional trade publications dragged their feet as first-mover VerticalNet moved so fast. "Why, would anyone with a century-old, 40-percent-pretax-margin business walk to the edge of a cliff, strap explosives around their body, hit the trigger, and dive off in flames into a zero-percent-pretax-margin business called the Internet, all voluntarily?" Walsh doesn't "blame" traditional print companies for not making the Internet leap, for not facing what he identifies as a fact of the present and future marketplace—that an Internet "business with no proven earnings potential can be the death knell for them."

For a quick insight into the difference in mind-set, Walsh pinpoints Internet thinking. It's in real time, not weekly or monthly, but now. "You can tell a publisher is still printcentric, not Net-centric, if you go to their site and it has last week's issue because the next issue hasn't come out yet." He makes a tough-minded prediction that in five years a number of professional trade publishing companies "won't be around. . . . those that don't reach out to Internet-centric companies and form partnerships or don't debrand their current product and create their own Internet divisions are going to have a tough time maintaining profitable businesses."

Hagan adds his revealing insight into why a bricks-and-mortar company is weighed down by a persistent past that dominates its present.

> *Traditional print companies are run by smart people, but it's a long way from the voice at the top saying we're going to change to the people executing those decisions. The voice from the top gets very faint when you get down to the field level where they earn their bonuses and make their salary based on how many ads they sell in the print book. It's not based on how many revenue dollars are flowing through the web site. So they're not going to cannibalize the primary product that they're out there selling. Any investment in the Web for a print company will come at the expense of earnings. So, their investments bleed their earnings. Whereas if you're a dot-com company, you're not just permitted, but you're almost rewarded for losing money. Because it's the cheapest market share that you'll ever gain. It's almost an unfair fight, but then we didn't write the rules, we're just exploiting them.*

When Walsh joined VerticalNet, it had a market valuation of $6 million compared with the $1.3 billion it would reach as the word got out on Wall Street. What Walsh describes as "a hell of a ride" had its roots in what impressed him and induced him to come on board from an AOL job with great stock options. It's a parable with a moral for all entrepreneurial start-ups.

> *I met the two guys who founded this company a couple of years before and number one, they had zero ego. Number two, they had a complete commitment to get the best guys on the bench, men and women to grow the company as fast as you can possibly grow it.*

> *They didn't have the ego of being the founder, of being king and getting in the way of building the best company that they could possibly build. Founders can think companies stay the same no matter how big or small. Companies change, they're living organisms. These guys had very healthy egos and were not overcome with a sense of their brilliance. They're very, very focused and out to make this the best company they could. I was instantly struck by the fact that they could build a company that was perfectly timed, perfectly focused, and perfectly aimed at what was going to be the ultimate winner in the Internet, business-to-business communities.*

America Online, Walsh points out, grasped the notion of community in its successful surge to the top of its marketplace, as did McNulty from his sales experience. It's not about technology. It's about community, particularly in the specialized businesses where McNulty made his mark. In the inner-directed world of specialists, there is a well-defined community of buyers and sellers who know each other, see each other at trade shows, play golf together, exchange tips and information, feel at home with each other. The community was already there. The Internet came along to provide what is now a familiar medium of communication, connection, exchange, and here-and-now interaction.

Walsh put his finger on what VerticalNet was doing. "The core competency of this business is to build industrial communities, focusing on a community and drilling down deep, deep, deep to the industry's needs, goals, information needs, and transaction capacity. It's a double-edged core competency—knowing how to share technology, software, marketing, and audience development across all our web sites. What this company does well is leverage expenses that it spends wisely across all its communities to share synergistically the cost of running all its web sites."

Not only can members of the same specialist community stay in touch, but they discover each other on a global scale. Early in the life of VerticalNet, buyers and sellers were finding each other in a way that previously was impossible. Such was the kind of contact made between a marketing director selling a centifruge that spins chemical compounds at higher speeds and an Australian factory of a European pharmaceutical company. Without the Internet and VerticalNet, they would not have known about each other and there would have been no million-dollar sale. As Walsh says, "there may be only 40 people who do a search for an esoteric topic like reverse osmosis in a given day, but we want to own all of them."

It's about the Internet as enabler, once a strange wonderland, now a standard medium that still arouses McNulty's enthusiasm. "From the start, companies could pay us a fee to build a storefront that generates sales leads throughout the year, kind of 'all you can eat.' Today you can buy books and videos and also hard hats on our web sites. We've added industrial auctions. We've made a deal which gives us hundreds of millions of dollars in inventory in used process equipment for the various industries we're in. We've got communities of buyers that we connect informationally. As we make a transition into connecting them transactionally, the revenue potential is staggering."

Hagan, the business visionary, adds: "We're going to be the dominant brand." Walsh, their enthusiastic third man, cheers them on. "All great ideas are simple. This company is based on a simple idea. As long as we keep it simple, we've got a fantastic bunch of years ahead of us."

3

CHRISTINA JONES—pcOrder
"Such a Great Opportunity"

3

CHRISTINA JONES—pcORDER

"Such a Great Opportunity"

In 1993, 24-year-old Christina (Christy) Jones had a multi-million-dollar conversation with Joe Liemandt, a fellow founder of a booming software company, Trilogy. It was about her idea for buying and selling computer products online and also about money—her Trilogy shares that were worth several million dollars.

She was determined to pursue her idea: an online business to streamline sales and distribution in the labyrinthine world of computer manufacturers, distributors, resellers, and retailers. From microchips to monitors, the products involve a staggering swirl of products and prices. "People put their toe in the water and saw that this isn't a pool, it's an ocean," Christy says.

Liemandt offered to back Christy's determination to start a new enterprise with Trilogy's technology and funds and to give her a substantial share in it, *if* she accepted an "all or nothing" offer. She had to give back her shares in Trilogy, "all she had," as he emphasizes. He had his entrepreneurial reason: "I wanted to make sure she really believed in her idea. I told her it had to be all or nothing."

Christy saw his point. "He wanted to make sure that I was very incented [*sic*] to wake up every morning and make the new organization successful, that I wasn't going to just rest on the millions I already had in Trilogy. It wasn't just an experiment."

So she didn't blink at the offer, but not as a bet-the-bank gambler. Not by a long shot. She was convinced that her idea would succeed and the start-up opportunity was something she couldn't turn down. As far as she was concerned, she wasn't making a bet. She was investing in herself.

> *I'm pragmatic. I'm not the type of person who goes to Vegas and takes all my winnings and doubles down on the roulette wheel. Here is how I looked at my decision. "I'm still really young. I've got a chance to build something, to be president of a company." Just the value of the learning to me was so high that I felt even if it didn't work out and even if I didn't have the Trilogy shares, I'd be able to make it up in the future if I needed to. That was my gut feeling. I didn't really worry—the value of the learning and the experience was so high. Now, if I had a family of four people that I was feeding and financial security rated as a very high goal for me, it would have been a much more difficult decision and I would have felt that it was a lot riskier. For me at that time, there was no way that I would walk away from a chance to build a company based on my idea. It was such a great opportunity.*

Rather than risk taker, opportunity seeker defines the remarkable career of a woman who has been singled out by *Forbes* magazine as "one of the nation's smartest young software entrepreneurs." *Information Week* has added the accolade of "Web Innovator," while *Working*

Woman selected her as one of the "Top 20 Leaders Under 30." As entrepreneur, she has identified, then pursued opportunities as college student, cofounder of a successful software company (Trilogy) and founder of another successful software company (pcOrder). The parallel theme of her career is the proverbial commitment to hard work, which undoubtedly helps to account for so much accomplishment while still in her 20's.

At pcOrder, Christy's goal was and is hardly modest: to transform the way personal computers are sold by creating an all-encompassing database that's easy to access. Christy's ongoing aim and intention is nonstop expansion: "Every day we're figuring out how to break down barriers and we're never satisfied with the status quo. We're always trying to push ahead and make things better. There are a lot of very smart people in our company, but it's not necessarily raw brains that makes the difference. Really hard work and attitude are a lot of it."

As is typical with Internet enterprises, the idea and the opportunity sprang into action quickly. On July 1, 1993, Christy's organization, pcOrder, began as a separate business unit within Trilogy. In June 1996, it became a separate company. In February 1999, it went public with 15 percent of its shares and raised $47 million.

Revenues grew from $10 million in 1997 to $21.7 million in 1998 and kept on growing. For the first quarter of 1999, revenues of $7.7 million increased 70 percent over the comparable quarter a year before and in the second quarter $8.9 million in revenues surpassed the previous year's quarter by 75 percent. Even though pcOrder was still not making money, it passed the stock market litmus test of IPO fever. On the first day, its offering price of $21 more than doubled. As for Christy, the nongambler, the first day's trading put her pcOrder holdings at $22.4 million. The $47 million raised in the public offering was a vote of confidence and a source of funds for further expansion. It also placed the total market value of pcOrder at $700 million.

The Christy Jones success story only becomes plausible in the context of the online transformation of the global economy. She went from an economics undergraduate who only knew the rudiments of programming to an important player in the computer industry, from a college student who worked in a department store after her freshman year to a company president who deals on an equal basis with the top executives of billion-dollar corporations. All this by her mid-20s.

There was also a conscious decision by the daughter of a Santa Barbara surgeon. In high school, she had been a typical student who enjoyed growing up in California, played tennis, and took ballet lessons. Then at 19, while in college, she recalls saying to herself: "Look, you can either go out with your friends and have fun and have a social life, or you can have work, but you can't have both. I chose work because I knew it would ultimately make me happier." By the time Christy graduated she had added a postscript to the work decision. She wanted to have a "real impact" and knew where she wanted to turn. She was "intrigued" by the software industry where she could travel on the fast track where she wanted to be.

> *The software industry changed all the rules of opportunity. If you went into management consulting, there's a clear path. You waited a certain number of years before you could get to certain levels of responsibility. In the software industry, you had the chance to make it big quickly if you hit. Actually, I was not that technical. I took computer science classes and then in the early days of Trilogy I was a programmer. But I became more involved in technical selling. I'd meet with customers and I'd build a prototype. It was customer-centered engineering.*

Christy and pcOrder followed in the footsteps of Trilogy, which had benefitted from a gap in the age of information. While companies had automated and computerized manufacturing, administration, and research and development (R&D), they had left out sales and marketing. In those areas, they were largely stuck in pen-and-paper, face-to-face processes that were inefficient, error prone, and unable to provide customization or expanded computer choice. Trilogy developed software to fill the gap and automate sales and marketing for major companies that have myriad models, parts, and products. It enables companies to work efficiently, quickly, and reliably in their sales and marketing operations.

By converting from paper to electronic files in a centralized database, companies can place at the disposal of their sales and marketing people a very sophisticated browser to access whatever information they need to put together an order. While Trilogy focused on serving the information needs of major companies in all industries, Christy followed up with her idea—to focus on the computer industry and provide a single database for the entire industry. pcOrder would draw on Trilogy's technology as well as its financial backing.

It was not the first demonstration of Christy's talent for finding opportunities, starting with an investment club she joined while at Stanford University. She calls it a matter of "being in the right place at the right time and a little bit of luck, actually a lot of luck."

I joined an investment club with Joe Liemandt and two of the other founders of Trilogy. We elected him president of the club and I was excited to work with him because I thought he understood a lot about stocks. I ran for and was made secretary of the club and worked with him as an officer of this club. I also got to know more about his project—the software business he was developing on the side.

During my sophomore year, I was talking to him about summer opportunities. I had worked in a department store the previous summer. I said to Joe that I didn't know anything about software, but it would be my dream and passion to work in a software company for the summer and for it to turn into more than that. I said I'll do whatever it takes to learn how to program. I think he just saw drive and spirit. It certainly wasn't for anything I had accomplished. He saw that I was ready to work really hard.

On his part, Joe had a single-minded goal: to start a software company. He was on an obsessive journey of research to learn about software companies, how they got started, what they did, how they operated. He was looking for a point of entry and he found it in the sales process and in the significant amount of company budgets spent on sales and marketing—a process typically handled the old-fashioned way. Salespersons struggled with hefty inventory manuals and sweated through consultations with company engineers to get everything right, matching parts and adjusting prices accordingly.

By his senior year, Joe was going all-out, in collaboration with three other students (including Christy), to develop software to computerize that process. He also soon learned he wasn't the only one in a development race that included major computer companies. He didn't need to be reminded that in the online world those who hesitate are in the wrong business. Joe is also a risk taker who delights in going to Las Vegas to hit the crap tables with his Trilogy teammates. So it was in character for him to quit school at the age of 21 as a Stanford University senior soon to graduate in June 1990.

The phone call to his parents announcing his decision shocked them. Parents don't send their sons and daughters to expensive, prestigious colleges so that they can drop out at the last minute to start a software company. The response from his father, a successful businessman, was blunt: "You're a moron!"

One of the original five dropped out of Stanford with Joe, while the other three (including Christy) juggled school and all-night programming sessions to develop what would became Trilogy, which less than six years after Joe dropped out was valued as high as $1 billion (having also won parental applause and affirmation).

In transforming the cumbersome and unwieldy task of processing orders for products—or sales configuration, as it is known—Joe and company developed a software to tie together all the information in inventory manuals by drawing on what they had learned at Stanford: sophisticated approaches involving rule-based programming, constraint-based equations, algebraic algorithms, and object-oriented programming. The Trilogy solution enables salespersons to sit down with customers and pull together a company's products from myriad sources to meet unique customer needs, then come up with a price that takes into account the many variations wanted. Salespersons can do even more. They can check on whether what's configured works with the customers' existing hardware.

In the process of building Trilogy's customer base, Christy identified another market for Trilogy's core technology for tracking, matching, and configuring computer products. Trilogy was primarily selling its software to major corporate users. Why not provide the entire computer industry with the same means of configuring products? Why not use the Trilogy software and technology to create a network for computer distribution that delivered instant communication, multivendor product configuration, and pricing? Why not? Hence her determination to set up pcOrder and her immediate acceptance of the all-or-nothing offer.

She identifies pcOrder as "very evolutionary from what we'd been doing at Trilogy."

> *I can't think of one "aha" moment. Trilogy was much more revolutionary than pcOrder. In the early days of working on Trilogy, we were seeing the opportunities and we had high hopes for building the next great software company. We did create something that was quite great and from that I saw the opportunity for pcOrder.*
>
> *At Trilogy, we were already working with HP [Hewlett-Packard] and IBM as well as Boeing, Silicon Graphics, and Alcatel, among others. We realized at Trilogy that we were working to solve each company's sales and distribution problems individually. Solve HP's, solve IBM's, etc. Regarding the computer industry, we realized that we needed to help manage the "ocean" of content across the whole computer industry. The solution was to build an industrywide database on top of Trilogy technology and create pcOrder, to create some order out of the disorder. We now have companies that are using both Trilogy and pcOrder. IBM, for example. It's using Trilogy for some of their mainframe products and using pcOrder for all of their PC and printer product lines.*

In harnessing the power of information for the provider of that power (the computer industry), pcOrder has built a know-it-all database. It's like handing reference librarians a single source for every dictionary, encyclopedia, and bibliography to be found in libraries all over the country and throwing in the ultimate browser that can select, mix, and match every piece of information that fits a very specific premise—with a few clicks of the mouse. It's a compelling combination of maximum information and minimum effort.

pcOrder makes it possible to draw on the power and speed of the computer and the limitless reach of the Internet to get the most out of information in buying and selling computer products. It enables corporate customers as paying subscribers to pcOrder to configure just the computer they want, which, for example, could be a Compaq computer with memory from Kingston and a printer from Hewlett-Packard linked to a server from IBM. Prices can be compared, compatibility of parts checked. With a few clicks of a mouse, pcOrder subscribers can check the most comprehensive database in the industry, 600,000 different parts from 1,000 manufacturers. Configuration of parts is the name of the game, compatibility the aim, the best deal the goal.

Christy's original idea was to create a central web site as a one-stop source of information and sales for the entire computer industry, with pcOrder acting as sales agent and getting a commission for every sale. However, that was going too far for distributors and for computer companies. Distributors and resellers saw themselves being cut out of the selling process. Computer companies saw erosion in their margins with the additional commissions.

Faced with industry resistance, Christy made a crucial and successful adjustment. pcOrder became an information provider and a source of linkage for manufacturers, distributors, and resellers to configure, price, and sell products over the Web. They could turn to pcOrder for software applications, product information, and connections with partners, then make their own decisions and buying arrangements. What Trilogy was doing for major companies, which produced and configured myriad products and parts in various high-tech companies, pcOrder made available for companies across the computer universe. Trilogy offered to turn an individual company's catalogs into easily accessible electronic files. pcOrder offered to turn myriad catalogs of computer companies into electronic files.

In its marriage of that content and the technology to access it, pcOrder offers a family of software applications designed to increase the automation of sales, marketing, and distribution. Each is available as a packaged application or can be customized for customers. pcOrder is out to serve everyone involved in sales and marketing in the computer industry, specifically manufacturers, distributors, resellers, integrators, retailers, and end users, including corporate buyers. A rundown of the available pcOrder software shows how Christy has covered all bases.

> *Catalog*—Users can easily search, browse, and compare products from pcOrder's catalog/database. For example: *Display all laptop computers with hard drives larger than one gigabyte.*
>
> *Configuration*—Put in the features you want and up come the components that can fit together.
>
> *Pricing*—Pricing information is customized to what the user wants, taking into account reseller costs from distributors.
>
> *Ordering*—Manufacturers, distributors, and resellers can order online and receive confirmations.
>
> *Referral*—Customers can be lined up with resellers who match their needs and wants, including the right location.
>
> *Finance*—Electronic movement of information provides information on leasing and buying, credit and financing to expedite the sales process.
>
> *Promotion*—Targeted promotions can be developed for specific customer groups to reduce excess inventory and improve profit margins.

Since keeping up with information technology is her business, Christy must always come up with new offerings, such as ContentSource, which capitalizes on pcOrder's position as the industry's largest collection of multivendor information. That translates into access to more than 100 product attributes for more than 100,000 products. Shoppers at stores and at portal sites can sit there and generate side-by-side comparisons of products, access product glossaries, and look at full-color images.

In Christy's all-out competitive strategy, she's also on the lookout for partnerships and alliances to "solidify our position as an e-commerce leader in moving the computer industry to the Web." In the case of Ingram Micro Inc, one of the world's largest wholesale distributors of technology products and services, a strategic partnership allows the company to license pcOrder content and technology. This will link, for the first time, their buyers, sellers, and assemblers of major brand-name PC manufacturers (including Compaq, IBM, Hewlett-Packard, and private label PCs) in a seamless e-commerce system. Ingram Micro's vast network of resellers can order custom-configured PCs from the company's extensive component inventory. It will save time and money.

In another partnership, pcOrder joined up with Active Research to work together to develop products and pursue sales and marketing. In the case of Compaq Computer, a joint alliance delivers e-commerce solutions to customers and resellers worldwide. pcOrder's technology platform, content services, and order network will help power Compaq's global e-commerce operations.

Christy sees the mid-1999 deal with Compaq as confirmation of what pcOrder can achieve: "This alliance demonstrates pcOrder's ability to power premier computer portals worldwide. Working this closely with the world's leading computer manufacturer broadens the reach of pcOrder's technology and content, and solidifies our position as an e-commerce leader in moving the computer industry to the Web."

When IBM set up an online store, pcOrder was in its favorite role as invisible enabler. Visitors to the store shop across the spectrum of IBM products—PCs, notebooks, servers, workstations, networking options, accessories, and software. They compare pricing at retailers and resellers and recalculate prices as they add or subtract options. If online shoppers choose a configuration that doesn't work or isn't available, a "traffic light" turns red. If it's green, the shopper indicates whether he or she wants to buy and is then directed to a site to complete the order. In the background, pcOrder is providing the pricing and the information on availability.

Christy, in the process of responding and adjusting to the marketplace, describes herself as "glued" to the Internet and reading "tons of magazines." But for her the "whole key" is hiring "people smarter than yourself" and continuously interacting with them: "There's no way that one person can keep on top of what's happening." What emerges in her reflections is the importance of flexibility to survive in the competitive and rapidly changing world of the Internet. There's no staying in one place, a lesson she's learned and recommends to all start-up entrepreneurs.

> *I think the most important thing when you're starting out is to realize that you must be willing to make trade-offs. Be prepared to change courses a lot of different times. Most importantly, make sure you're an expert on whatever you're doing. Because if you're an expert and really understand your market, good ideas will come to you. You'll figure out where the real holes are in the marketplace. You need to write a business plan, but you shouldn't spend too much time on it because I guarantee that you'll bring it out a year later and laugh. The high-level vision in a business plan*

may be 95 percent accurate, but all the details on how you actually achieve that vision will be 100 percent in the other direction.

If you ask about our core competency at pcOrder, I would say it's our commitment to map the way industry works with software. So it's not just the pure programming, it's more the application of it. It's understanding how people really want to buy things and how they really sell things. Or understanding their manufacturing problems and giving them a complete solution. I'm not technical, and I didn't have the business background, but what I did learn from the Trilogy experience is to persevere, to wake up every morning trying to break down the barriers. And then the whole key of hiring the best people, people that are smarter than you are. Then interact with them continuously.

Nothing demonstrates Christy's hiring acumen like her 1996 coup in bringing on board computer industry innovator and Computer Hall of Fame inductee Ross Cooley as her company's chair and CEO. It was a brilliant stroke. The up-and-coming young software entrepreneur teamed up with a seasoned and accomplished executive with contacts and prestige throughout the PC world. He opens doors in the industry, giving her the opportunity to earn the respect of senior executives, forcing them to look beyond the youthful entrepreneur to her company and what it has to offer.

Christy has no qualms about being a company founder who turns over two key positions to someone else. Not for her is the temptation of trying to do everything herself and to be all things for all aspects of her business. She met Cooley on a business visit to Compaq Computer in trying to drum up business for pcOrder. She was in the selling role, he in the buying position. As senior vice president and general manager of Compaq for North America, he ran the company's $7 billion operation in the United States and Canada. He saw a bright, determined entrepreneur with a great idea. She saw a personable, impressive executive who had built strong relations with industry executives during his 12 years at Compaq, which followed 18 years at IBM. Here was yet another opportunity.

In a variation of her all-or-nothing conversation with Joe Liemandt, Christy would offer Ross, for whom retirement was on the near horizon, a chance to earn a dollar a year for four years—and profit handsomely if pcOrder was a success. He would own a 7 percent share in the company, which amounted to more than Christy's own 4.8 percent share. (As it turned out, Ross's shares soared to $29 million in the first IPO day, compared with Christy's $22.4 million.) She has no doubt that it was a great move.

> *In turning over two key positions of chairman and CEO, I really viewed it as adding more talent to the team as opposed to taking anything away. It was a once-in-a-lifetime opportunity to get somebody like Ross on board, especially with what we're trying to do, being so focused on the computer industry. It was really important that we had somebody from the industry that people could relate to and feel really understood their problems, somebody who had lived through the problems. He added so much to our team and to our feasibility as a company. He also has opened up many more opportunities for me personally. So, I've looked at the move as much more a matter of helping pcOrder excel as well as opening up opportunities for me rather than a matter of having to sacrifice any titles.*

In action, the Jones-Cooley team has developed in textbook fashion. Christy handles the day-to-day operations, focusing on new products, initiatives, operating priorities, and recruiting (the company has grown from 30 to 250 employees). She works on aligning different groups within the company to make sure that development is in sync with sales, oversees finances, handles forecasting and financial management, and deals with the media. On top of that, she logs 100,000 miles a year on American Airlines to keep up with the industry and to join Ross on company visits. He focuses on what customers need and want and on the investment community. Christy describes the informal division of responsibilities as "largely external" for Ross and "more internal" for me. "When we disagree," she adds, "we talk it through and try to see both sides of the picture. We have always been able to work things through and come up with a better answer."

> *When we first started pcOrder, we were very chaotic and Ross suggested that we have managers' meetings. He suggested getting the company's key people together once a week to talk about key decisions. When we met with customers, I would talk about the software and a vision of what the technology could do. Ross would help map out the technology in terms of the customers' business problems.*

Where it counts they turned out to be a formidable combination. *Forbes* magazine has described them as an "impressive pair: he, the smooth industry veteran who can charm open the doors of boardrooms; she, the demure-seeming entrepreneur with cover-girl looks who packs an intellectual wallop."

Cooley recalls one of their first joint sales visits to the CEO of a computer manufacturing company with tens of billions in sales. The CEO liked the software for sales configuration that they were offering, but he didn't want to buy a license. He wanted to buy the whole company. Christy responded that it wasn't for sale. He answered that "at the right price point" everyone will sell. Christy—whose company had 39 employees and was grossing at the time only $1 million a quarter—looked him straight in the eye and said, "One billion dollars."

The CEO laughed and said, "You've got a high opinion of your potential."

"I think I'm right," Christy answered.

Drawing on his long years of experience, Ross provides a veteran's firsthand assessment of Christy in action:

> *She does her homework and when she makes up her mind that she's correct, she's very persuasive. She's afraid of nothing. She has no fear in her. I've been with her numerous times when she's looked CEOs of multi-billion-dollar companies in the eye and said, "Take my offer now or take it later." What Christy understood was that the distribution systems that the industry had created were extremely expensive, slow, and that it was just a matter of time before someone would deliver better information, much quicker, and at lower cost with electronic commerce. One reason why electronic commerce has been so quickly adopted in the computer industry is that the majority of computer companies have spent most of the '90s converting their business processes to build-to-order instead of build-to-forecast.*
>
> *With Christy, number one was her vision of the revolution that would occur in the buying and selling of technology products. Number two was her conviction that she's correct. When I first met her, it was obvious to me that she was either going to be successful or flame out. My comment to my colleagues at Compaq was that she was wise beyond her years. For someone with her limited amount of experience, she had*

talked to enough people that had experience and had thought things through to the point where she had a very logical answer for every challenge she received. She's a competitor and a winner who has the ability to galvanize people to execute her vision and her ideas.

Both in her personal and her entrepreneurial life Christy takes a "long-term view" that puts work in its place, starting with an update on her "work mode."

I've just been willing to work hard. I was willing to sacrifice 10 years of other things—not everyone would make that decision. I was willing not to have a social life, not travel, not have vacations, work all the time. But I loved it, so in general it was not a sacrifice to me. When people call me an entrepreneur and a risk taker, I always feel a little bit awkward, like it's almost an undue compliment because I don't really feel like a risk taker.

While I've loved being totally focused on work for the last 10 years, I know that's not how I'll live the rest of my life. I kind of look at life as not being balanced all at the same time, but being balanced in terms of your entire life. Working like crazy over the last 10 years has given me the opportunity to build a great team. I can start stepping back a little bit. I still work very hard and love working, but other things can start entering into my life whether it be travel or getting in shape, or a social life. And at some point, I expect that I'll have a family or hope that I'll have a family and that will add other aspects to my life.

As for pcOrder, she is looking toward a limitless future for the company, behind the scenes but universally and globally present in the buying and selling of computer products in line with the company's registered trademark, "Moving the computer industry to the Web." There is a vision and a goal.

> *The goal we would like is that every single time you buy a computer or go to get information on a computer as an end buyer, pcOrder would be there behind the scenes. Whether you're on Compaq's web site or you went to CompUSA and into a kiosk in their store, or you went to a web site to run an RFP [request for proposal], pcOrder would provide you with the ability to configure the system, figure out what works together, get all the information about the parts that meet your needs, determine the price, determine when you could get it, and actually place the order. The grand vision is to have pcOrder technology and content involved in every computer bought.*

WILLIAM PORTER &
CHRISTOS COTSAKOS—E*TRADE

"Go for It"

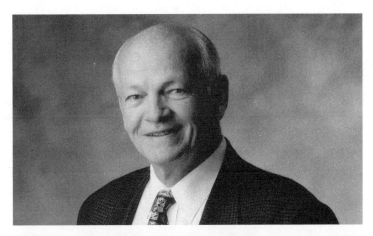

Top, *William Porter;* bottom, *Christos Cotsakos.*

WILLIAM PORTER &
CHRISTOS COTSAKOS—E*TRADE

"Go for It"

At 6 A.M. on a Monday, an East Coast CEO and a California high-tech inventor/entrepreneur met for breakfast at a Hyatt hotel in Palo Alto. The 1996 meeting was a detour by the CEO as a favor to a recruiter friend who was headhunting for the Californian's online company. When coffee was poured, the East Coast visitor was more polite than curious. He had never heard of the inventor and, besides, he didn't have financial services experience. For his part, the Californian was skeptical about the visitor's credentials. They sounded "too good to be true."

William (Bill) Porter met Christos Cotsakos.

Successful inventor (Porter) met highly touted executive (Cotsakos). The post–World War II generation met the Vietnam generation. Committed technologist met savvy high-energy CEO. Bill was looking for a "world-class leader" to take over his company, E*TRADE, originally founded in 1992 to handle stock trades for such companies as Schwab and Fidelity. Christos was eager to get on with a busy day.

Then something happened. A pro forma breakfast that was supposed to last only an hour lasted three days. Christos recalls the encounter. "We talked primarily about ideas—then politics, the military, corporate governance, economics, and leadership. We talked about everything—what he wanted to do, what I wanted to do. Then it blurs. Bill and I laugh about our first encounter."

Christos, his curiosity aroused, proceeded to put off the company waiting to sign him up in favor of 72 hours of talking to Bill and his people at E*TRADE. Meanwhile, a cautious Bill was checking out Christos's credentials.

> *Christos seemed too knowledgeable, too outstanding. Unreal. I asked him to visit the company's offices to talk with our management team and other executives. At the end of the day, we agreed to talk some more. And we did. Christos spent most of the next day chatting with just about everybody in the company. Then he came into my office in the afternoon and said, "Bill, here's what you have. Here are the strengths, the weaknesses, the issues, the challenges that I foresee today, and in the future, for this company." He was right, across the board. He's outstanding.*
>
> *After that, he talked with our directors, and at least one of them came back with the same reaction that I had. So I said, "Well, get more references," which we did. The references were presidents and vice presidents, chairmen and CEOs, board members. When they found out we were calling about Christos, every one of them came through and asked, "What do you want to know?" They all said, "If you can get him, you've got a winner." And they were absolutely, positively correct.*

Both men took a risk. Bill was going against the conventional wisdom and advice that his company needed someone with a background in finance. Christos's most trusted friends said he was "crazy" to think of acting on his "epiphany" and accepting a CEO job at an unproven start-up in a very crowded and competitive industry.

> *I would be turning down another seven-plus-digit salary for an unknown compensation package. Most of my friends thought I was nuts. They were stunned when I told them I was leaning towards the start-up. People that I trust and rely on advised me not to do it. On top of that, everybody was saying that we could not be successful. I was risking everything in my career and reputation. The advice of the day was if you jump ship (and do not take a job you should have taken)—and fail—you'll alienate a lot of people and kill your career. And there will not be a lot of places you'll be able to go after that.*
>
> *But Bill and I had a shared vision about what we could do for individual investors, giving them access to investing opportunities on a virtual playing field, level with large institutional investors—all of this was part of democratizing personal investing and demystifying the process. Our discussions were about ennobling ideas and enabling technology. It was out of the realm of what was the expected norm, grounded in a uniquely different space. I couldn't let this go. There was this energy and spiritualism. It was larger than life. There was a passion to make it work no matter what the odds. It was not about making money. It was about making a difference, both as an individual and as a member of a team.*
>
> *I just can't say enough about Bill for trusting me with his dream, and I know that Bill is very appreciative about my role in reinventing the company. We talked a lot about technology, about the system and how it needed to change. We talked about marketing,*

about what he would do and what I would do. When Bill made his offer, he said, "If we're going to work together, you're going to run this." When I said, "Let's be clear, you mean you'll let me do what I want to do," he answered, "I'm going to give you the keys to the car." How many people do you know who have been working on an idea, their own baby, for 14 years, and who turn it over to someone they've only known for 72 hours? Someone who tells you that they believe in you, just go do it. What a sense of responsibility, privilege, and pride that gives you! From there, we built such a bond between us—one that's unbreakable— much like two soldiers in the same foxhole fighting for their lives and their mission.

In joining personal risk to business opportunity, Christos identifies the entrepreneur in himself as a no-holds-barred CEO carrying on for Bill as company founder and chairman. "Bill founded the company. I reinvented it. Bill is a personal hero of mine who gave me the space to build on what he started. So many company founders are at loggerheads with people they bring in. Bill and I have never ever had that, even when we disagree."

When Cotsakos took over in 1996, E*TRADE was a small discount broker that had started out by offering stock trading via America Online (AOL) and Compu-Serve. What emerged in less than four years of aggressive expansion of E*TRADE under Christos is a company that is a global leader in online personal financial services. Its customers can invest in stocks, bonds, options, and IPOs and access services in banking, retirement planning, real estate, insurance, and taxes. As the world's most-visited online investing site, E*TRADE has built a customer base of more than 3 million and was rated (in the spring of 2000) the number one overall online broker by the leading rating system,

Gomez Advisors. It vaulted past 50 other online brokerages in the Gomez ratings and was second only to Schwab in volume, controlling 15 percent of the online brokerage market.

Under Christos's leadership, E*TRADE was on its way to becoming a "digital financial media company," setting as its goal involvement in every aspect of personal finances—from free, across-the-board financial information to a powerful financial hub to manage an individual's finances electronically. For good measure, after three stock splits, the company's market value vaulted from $50 million in March 1996 to $9.4 billion in March 2000.

First, there was Porter's entrepreneurial vision as founder.

> *In 1982, when I started TRADE*PLUS [the predecessor of E*TRADE], people absolutely didn't believe in the whole idea [of direct, discount financial transactions without going through brokers]. Everybody that I talked to thought I was crazy. In fact, all through the '80s my company was not successful at all. When the stock crash came in '87—[and] for the next two years—neither my technical guy who did most of the programming nor myself was paid. Just couldn't afford it. At times in that period I even had to loan the company $2,000 or $3,000 at the end of the month.*
>
> *In the late '80s, I got very serious about the Internet and tried to figure out how to get the company on it. Up until then, investors signed onto Telenet, a data network system, and reached us through that or CompuServe. When I tried to get onto the Internet, I was shot down. Commercial stuff wasn't wanted. When that roadblock broke up in 1992, E*TRADE was one of the first on the Internet.*

Then there was Christos's vision as entrepreneurial reinventor of E*TRADE, a vision that became clear in 72 hours of discussion.

The idea behind it all is that you can empower individuals with a powerful arsenal of actionable information. You need the combination of brokerage and banking as a base while adding all the other things surrounding financial services, from mortgages to insurance, from real estate to retirement. I envisioned a global financial exchange that would provide a personalized financial cockpit for everyone using the Internet. As a tool and a channel, you then brand the e-franchise as a trusted, secure, and private network.

Bill and I talked continuously about new ways to add different components to the site. It was an invigorating encounter between two very focused individuals about how they saw the world evolving. We were very strategic and at the same time very tactical on how to implement successfully our vision. Three mission-critical components were involved. There was the technological infrastructure—using the Internet both as tool and channel. There was the customer experience—making sure that it was simple, secure, and easy to use. There was the trusted brand—building one that would resonate with the lifestyle change taking place with the consumer. That was the convergence of our thinking. It came about as the great benefit of two entrepreneurs coming together. You get double vision in a good way.

Christos added action, fast action, at the speed of Internet deals. A prime example was another crucial meeting: this time a sushi dinner with Mitchell Caplan, CEO of Telebanc, the largest online bank. Another component was about to be added to the E*TRADE menu of financial offerings. The bank CEO from Arlington, Virginia, who was in California to discuss joint ventures with the likes of Yahoo!, had agreed to squeeze in a meal with Christos. Barely 15 minutes into the meal, Christos surprised Caplan with an offer that Telebanc didn't refuse. "Look," he said, "we want to cut a deal. Here's what we think should work." It was a stock-for-stock buyout of Telebanc, which Christos wanted to complete in a week. It took six days, a $1.8 billion deal in July 1999—and at that point the largest e-commerce acquisition in the high-flying history of the Internet. As far as Christos is concerned: "You can't be wed to what you've already done. The world is changing too fast. When you make a strategic move, you become an entrepreneur all over again and risk everything all over again. It's pretty nerve-racking. So, you gotta love it."

The acquisition announced less than four years after E*TRADE had begun Internet trading, highlighted a string of alliances and ownership deals. The alliances involved AOL as well as online companies in bond trading, credit cards, insurance, investment research, and financial news. Deals for partial ownership tied E*TRADE to online companies in electronic trading, loans, investment banking, stock clearance, and e-mail services. Christos added a family of mutual funds. In going head-to-head with online giants like Schwab, size is not what counts in the Christos strategy. It's being "adaptive, fast, and understanding and improving the customer's experience."

In 1997 and again in 1998, Christos went before his board of directors, Bill at his side, to propose major moves that reminded the directors that their CEO thrives on calculated risk taking. The directors swallowed hard, discussed the ramifications of what Christos planned to do and spelled out their concerns. Then he won them over.

I remember going to the board [in 1997] after eight quarters of profitability. Bill was so proud that the *company was profitable. I remember saying that I was now going to change our whole technological architecture, make a 360-degree turn and declare a moratorium on profits. We were going to move in a totally different direction. The board was thunderstruck! I wanted to transform us from an online brokerage site to a financial hub, where we would have free quotes for everybody and have both visitors and members. Access for the public would be free and we would start spending $300-plus million a year on advertising and on branding E*TRADE across a variety of media. We would build a whole new technology platform. I presented an outline of how it would work and how my team was going to execute the plan.*

I was chipping away for about four hours on why we should do this when Bill leaned over to me and whispered, "Go for it." At the end of six hours the board was enthusiastic and committed to the plan when we launched it. Our stock was in double digits when we announced the plan and it dropped to single digits shortly thereafter. We told the industry that in one year we would open up 1 million new accounts. We were laughed at, but we ended up opening 1.2 million accounts earlier than our target date. Ultimately, the stock went vertical—up to $140—and split twice.

In the middle of 1999, I told the board how we're going to reinvent the company again—through digital financial media. We were going to continue to spend on technology and marketing while adding multimedia. We were going to deliver video, voice, and data through both fixed and mobile platforms. It's a huge investment of $100-plus million. After a long discussion—another six hours with the both of us—Bill leaned over and whispered in my ear the three most seductive words in our vocabulary, "Go for it."

It's all about looking at your ideas in a grand way, but never being afraid to creatively destroy them. The key is to be directionally correct. You just can't be wed to what you've already done because the world is changing too fast. Each time you make changes in your ideas, you become an entrepreneur all over again.

Side by side, from one generation to the next, the two partners and their "double vision" as entrepreneurs demonstrate how wide open the Internet is and how it can wipe out traditional boundaries. Brokers and bankers, bond dealers and borrowers—any and all providers of financial services—can fit under the same company umbrella at E*TRADE. Christos calls it "convergence." Bill, who describes himself as "a real believer in the Internet," is certain that it will "change the way we do business across the board. . . . I don't care if you're talking steam engines or you're talking nylon socks and everything in between. Everything is going to be Internet impacted and every business has to accommodate to it. The Internet is becoming very quickly the most dislocating thing in terms of commerce in my lifetime."

The Internet also can bring together the most unlikely of partners, unlikely only if they are viewed in terms of traditional differences like age, background, training, and personal experiences. When the chemistry works and the outlooks match, the differences don't matter. In fact, they can contribute to entrepreneurial success. In the case of E*TRADE, the Internet brought together an inventor who has always focused on how things work and how to make them work better with a competition-driven businessman and dreamer who wants to change the rules and make a difference on a grand scale.

E*TRADE originated when stock quotes became available online and Bill wondered why "someone hadn't done it right" by providing information and services for investors. So he decided to do what he likes to do: start a company. Once, in filling out a biographical form, he summed up his pleasure in life as "launching and managing technologically based ventures to develop new products, services, and markets for the benefit of everyone involved." He calls it "fun." Starting in 1968, he proceeded to start up 20 companies. With E*TRADE, Bill has helped to write what he considers an obituary for traditional stock exchanges and brokerage firms: "Brokers, as we know them today, are going to die a very slow, agonizing death. It's not a career you want your children to go into. If you're sophisticated enough to use a computer, you're sophisticated enough to buy and sell stock yourself."

In reviewing what he's accomplished, Porter says, "Everything I've ever done has been based on technology." It's been fueled by his passion for improving the way things operate. His efforts have led to 14 patents in a lifetime of successful inventions. They include the first low-light TV camera for medical endoscopy, the first shoulder-mounted, backpack broadcast television camera for remote pickups, and the first exhaust sensors for automotive pollution control. In 1964, he drew on his experience working nights on the railroad to pay his college expenses in order to develop the first electronic checkout system for diesel-electric locomotives (still used by most major railroads). At one point, he led the development of an infrared horizon sensor for NASA. Faced with the problem of stabilizing the NASA nose cone, he came up with the solution—an infrared system that stays focused on the horizon.

In launching E*TRADE, Bill's track record made it easy to bring in start-up money from venture capitalists. His technological know-how was applied to the design of system architecture, which has enabled E*TRADE to keep adding products and services that respond to customer demand. All along, he has looked at the world as an inventor with the mind-set of a mathematician (a reflection of his major at Adams State College, Colorado), someone who "always just liked to do things differently." To fill out his personal portfolio, he added a master's degree in physics from Kansas State University and subsequently was a Sloan Fellow in management at the Massachusetts Institute of Technology. He served in the U.S. Navy from 1945 to 1947.

As to being an entrepreneur, Bill didn't realize that he was one until the late 1980s. "I was doing what entrepreneurs do—start new things. Most of it had been inside big companies where they got the benefits." At the companies—General Electric and Textro where he held management positions in research—he was heavily involved in military projects, some of which are still classified. In 1968, he changed course, starting his own company to market his inventions. After selling the company in 1974 to Warner Communications, he spent eight years starting up companies while consulting in microelectronics through the Stanford Research Institute.

He has not stopped entrepreneuring. His latest brainchild is the International Securities Exchange (ISE), an online options exchange to replace the floor-broker system, which he dismisses as antiquated. When he told his wife about the idea, her long-suffering reaction was, "You'll never quit, will you?" Nowadays, when asked repeatedly about what it takes to be an online entrepreneur, he sticks to basics.

> *I don't think being an entrepreneur is any different with the Internet. You have to do the same things. The options exchange that I'm working on [ISE] is not Internet related, other than the fact that there has been growth in the trading business because of the Internet and the E*TRADEs of the world. First of all, as an entrepreneur, you've got to do your homework*

until you're absolutely convinced that you're right. Then, you have to be prepared to change if necessary. At school, I was not a straight A student, never have been. But when I get an idea I'm dogged about it. Second, you have to persevere. It was 10 years before TRADE*PLUS or E*TRADE was a success. You must stay with your idea. Third, you must operate with integrity. Those are the guidelines that I think are important.

With Bill looking upon Christos as a "universe-class leader and manager" (to whom he has handed over E*TRADE's chairmanship) and with Christos looking upon Bill as one of his personal heroes and friends, their working partnership dramatizes what binds them as Internet entrepreneurs. Together, they combine a competitive spirit with an unwavering conviction that they are right in their view of the new world the Internet is creating. To act on their conviction, they recognize the need to think outside the box. Right off the bat, in searching for a CEO, Bill "turned down immediately" prospects that were high-powered players in the brokerage business. "I didn't want restrictive thinking in the company," he explains.

In gravitating to Christos, he found a CEO who was never a pure technologist and never had financial services experience but who had the same innate smartness and spirit of discovery—in spite of their differences in background. Bill, whose father was an electrical engineer for a public service company in Colorado, cut classes in high school to go to the library and learn by reading. Christos, whose father was an immigrant short order cook in New Jersey, came late to the learning game. He describes himself as a disinterested student who had "the attention span of a gnat on a nit, a maverick, untrainable, always restless, continuously bored with school." He preferred to run with his neighborhood gang until his parish priest got him off the streets and made him an altar boy. But it was the Vietnam War that really turned him around.

After managing to graduate from high school, Christos tried to get his life on track by becoming a pilot in the air force or the navy. He was turned down. Both services were looking for college graduates. So he ended up volunteering for Vietnam as the leader of a fire team with the 101st Airborne Infantry. It was total immersion in jungle and guerilla fighting, in survival and death, and in loyalty and commitment to a team. It was a transforming experience.

Severely wounded in action, he came home with a Purple Heart, a Bronze Star for Valor, an army commendation for valor, and an air medal, among others. He also returned with traumatic memories of close friends killed and wounded in battle, and with no career prospects. "It occurred to me through seeing all the killing and the destruction that if I ever got out alive, I was going to do something different with my life. I was going to make a difference with my family, my friends, and in the community. I was going to make use of myself as an instrument to do well and do things that could really be ennobling as a human being. Vietnam was a character-defining moment. For some 10 years after Vietnam, I suffered from survival guilt. I felt an honor-bound obligation to make something of myself because I came out of that war alive. So I dedicated myself to trying to make a difference and not let anybody or anything stand in my way."

When he tried to get a job at a bank, an interviewer who dismissed him as having nothing to offer turned him down. No college degree, no signs of talent, no skills. His experience as a fire team leader and decorated veteran was dismissed as worthless. The experience still rankles Christos. "I've disliked bank managers ever since," says chairman and CEO Christos, who eventually bought an $1.8 billion online bank. His next turndown came when he tried to get into college. His applications were rejected, and he only got in because of the helpful intervention of his brother, who drew on personal and political contacts. When the dean decided to give him a chance, he was in class the very day the door opened. He proceeded to apply himself for the first time, earning a degree with honors in political science and communications.

After graduation, he went west in pursuit of a theater career, barely supporting himself by guiding tours at Universal Studios for $1.45 an hour. So when Federal Express was starting out and advertising for cargo handlers at $3 an hour, he rushed right over, applied, and was turned down. He went back again and again until he finally talked the company into hiring him. From then, the transformation of the maverick gained momentum. He set out to learn things very fast so that he could get promoted, run things, and escape jobs or managers he disliked. "I viewed it as a great opportunity to continually do other things. By my second day, I was scheduling couriers and soon I was talking about scheduling airplane routes. I have always believed that you can do anything based on willpower and energy. I always believed if you believe you can make a difference, you will."

Christos worked hard, slept little (even today he reports that he sleeps less than four hours a night), and on the side earned a master's degree in business administration summa cum laude at Pepperdine University. In his 19 years with Federal Express, he kept rising until he became vice president and general manager for all operations in Europe, Africa, and the Near East. He was no longer turned down. He was in demand. In 1993, his talent for innovating global strategies caught the attention of the research firm, A.C. Nielsen, which recruited him to become president and chief operating officer for international business. In the next two years, he developed and expanded the company's international operations through acquisitions, partnerships, and new client relations. In March 1995, he became president, co-CEO, and chief operating officer. On the side, he became a doctoral candidate in economics at the University of London. He also has written a book on Internet investing, *It's Your Money,* and has a contract for two more.

Then he had breakfast with Bill Porter.

"I went from soldier to courier to researcher to entrepreneur," Christos says. "Each time, I was intimidated by what I didn't know and had to learn quickly." To keep on top of what's happening in the Internet world, he reads everything: newspapers, magazines, periodicals, and books. He reads or scans six to seven books a week. He roams the Internet for ideas and does a great deal of listening to people of all ages and at all levels. As a change of pace, he reads military biographies and accounts of military campaigns as well as poetry. For relaxation, he likes to watch old B movies and practice Japanese tea ceremony.

> *Listening is like putting your ear to the railroad track to see if the train's coming. You'd be surprised how smart people of all ages are. I learn a lot from kids. They look at the world differently, they are innocent and refreshingly nonpolitical. I learn from people viewed as senior citizens by listening to what they did in business, what affected them in their lives, what they would have done differently. One thing that most of them tell me is that they would worry less. So I try to worry less, and if I get into trouble, I try to figure out how things could have been done differently. I've always spent a lot of time in the trenches getting my hands dirty and I'm not afraid to say, "I don't know what the hell you're talking about. I don't know what this means." People*

take great pride in helping to educate you. So if you ask questions and use deductive reasoning, you'll learn continually from the people and environment around you.

As leader of an Internet company, Christos has adopted a management policy that he summarizes as "think big, act small, and move fast . . . very fast." He has a personalized version of what it means.

First of all, you have to dream about a vision that is magically larger than life, a vision that has benefits that are not just commercial, but really benefit humankind. You always have to think on a grand scale. But when you look at implementing your vision, you've got to break it down into small components and rapid deployment teams that are responsible for delivering the parts while integrating it into the grand scale. The last part is speed: moving fast, very fast. You must be willing to break the rules, make mistakes, try again, and reward people who have made directionally correct mistakes.

I give people a lot of space to succeed, I empower them, and hold them responsible and accountable for their actions. Leadership and decisions are distributed to whoever has the best expertise and is in the best position to make a contribution. I give people freedom: the freedom to think, to act, and to become financially independent so that they can make a difference in their personal and professional lives. I try to coach and counsel our people, while leading by example. I compensate them very well so that if they make a difference individually and through a team effort, they get monetary income as well as psychic income. However, in the end it's never about the money, it's about making a difference.

He also draws on his Vietnam experiences. "One of the things I learned is that if you go in halfway, you can't win. To be in the trenches you also need to have air cover. You've got to know when to bring in the heavy artillery. You've got to go out and say, 'I'm here, I've arrived, and I'm not going to be messed with.'" As on the battlefield, he keeps looking over his shoulder watching out for "competitors both day and night and staying paranoid all the time. . . . People are always on the lookout for profitable business models, and we've shown that you can make a lot of money doing what we're doing, so everybody's trying to figure out how to get a piece of the action. Staying paranoid all the time about everybody and everything keeps you focused." He keeps his own team on constant alert with his reputation for predawn phone calls and after-hours' updates on what's going on.

All the while, Christos maintains a 360-degree field of focus—"looking around and learning pieces from everything you see and implementing them in your plan." Bill describes Christos as being on constant alert for his greatest fear, the proverbial "two kids in the garage" who come up with the next big thing that revolutionizes the field of competition. Sitting in his command post at E*TRADE, Christos is surrounded in a crowded office by career mementos and three large, framed *Star Wars* movie posters. A prominent place on his cluttered desk is occupied by a three-story plastic toy garage, with two miniature plastic figures in its first floor. The gift garage arrived with a message that would comfort any Internet entrepreneur: "Are these the guys in the garage you've been worried about? Now you can relax. You own them." Given the all-out way Christos competes, the message is likely to become true to life—by merger, alliance, or acquisition.

GREGORY K. JONES—uBID, INC.

"Where the Customer Can Set the Price"

5

GREGORY K. JONES—uBID, INC.

"Where the Customer Can Set the Price"

At the age of 35, Gregory (Greg) K. Jones had notched yet another management success, this time as a top business development officer at APAC, a call center outsourcing firm in Deerfield, Illinois, where he was the key mover in the company's explosive growth. In less than two years at the company, he had played a role in growing revenue from $100 to $276 million annually. In 1996, APAC was the top IPO for Merrill Lynch and tagged the fourth fastest growing company in the United States by *Forbes* magazine.

Then the phone rang and he was invited to discuss an online venture that at the time was an idea in search of someone to run with it. Creative Computers, a California computer retailer and direct marketer, had already tried to recruit him for a top management position. He had refused. This time, Creative Computers made an entrepreneurial offer he couldn't refuse, but certainly not because of what the company put on the table: a chance to take a two-thirds cut in his $450,000 compensation plan to run a start-up company with an initial employee roll of three programmers. The offer came with backing for the launch, but no guarantees. If the business succeeded, Jones succeeded, thanks to stock options (which could only be exercised after five years). If his "big risk" failed, he would still have done "the only thing I've ever wanted to do—run companies."

It was the *idea* on the conference table that he couldn't refuse.

> *I was so excited about the idea. It could never happen quite this way until the Internet—where the customer can set the price. The idea was to sell from business to consumer in an auction environment. This idea that customers could set their own price in buying from businesses was revolutionary. I couldn't get it out of my mind. Two-way communication involving everyone in the world is phenomenal. I think it's such a great thing. The idea hit me and I said to myself: This is it.*

Greg did insist on one condition, the location of company headquarters in Silicon Prairie rather than Silicon Valley. He and his wife, Karin, wanted to continue living in the Chicago area and raise their two little daughters there. Hence the company's Elk Grove Village, Illinois, location. Even this he insists is good for business by enabling him to recruit high-quality talent where the bidding is not what it is in talent-hungry California. Like Greg, his key people come on board more for the challenge and the stock options than for the salaries. "We have been able to attract people that I don't think we could have if we had been on the West Coast," Greg says. "There are so few companies like ours in the Chicago area that we have an opportunity to attract great people."

For Greg, the offer from California was like offering a baseball fan the chance to recruit and manage his own big-league team. It suited his temperament as a consumer and his mind-set as a business executive. "I love the idea of being able to say how much I want to pay and I hate thinking I got ripped off." Appropriately, the company was called uBid and it became Greg's big chance to do what he always wanted. "I'm really an entrepreneur at heart and from the beginning this was going to be a separate business. The parent company was just going to fund it. I was going to run it."

Like other online entrepreneurs, he had spotted the connection between the Internet and an idea that can deliver value to the customer and profits to the provider. Early in the online phenomenon, he was responding to what the *Economist* magazine identified three years later as what "may be one of the most valuable innovations wrought by the Internet"—online auctions (projected to reach $19 billion by 2003). This particular auction would take a different approach from eBay, which pioneered online auctions with person-to-person online trading. The new company would be a business-to-customer online auction house, same basic formula, different piece of the action. Its focus is on idle inventory, which threatens optimum use of assets and penalizes a company's bottom line. Here was a chance for companies to shed the inventory albatross: obsolescence of products displaced by newer and improved versions. Management could make room for better-selling products and avoid inventory costs, which extend from damage, spoilage, and pilferage to maintenance and administrative expenses. In many states, companies face property taxes on their inventories, as well.

In sizing up the opportunity, Greg pinpoints the connection between the idea and the pressures on companies and then the role of Creative Computers in the start up of uBid:

> *We specialize in excess, overstock, and refurbished product. That traditionally is product that major man-*

ufacturers are looking to move, not through their main-stream channels but through an alternate channel or alternate distribution channels. And we find that they're looking to move that product very, very quickly, which means the auction format is ideal for that situation.

A couple of things helped us get started. First of all, we were very determined in what we wanted to do. Second, our parent company had a lot of back-end systems already in place, and so we were able to move quickly. Third, we've been very aggressive in our marketing and our emphasis on building a big company. I'd say we had the guts to go for it. We sent out a bunch of direct mail pieces and we sent e-mails. Drawing on the big customer file of our parent company, we said, "Hey, check us out." Companies came and checked us out and that's how we got started. It was a total start from scratch. For six months, three programmers, three others, and I worked seven days a week to get online and it was only then that I started to hire other people.

Merchandising vice president Tim Takesue, who joined uBid as it was going online, describes Jones in action during the launch and ever since. "I've worked with other CEOs in the past and have never met anybody who is as hard driving and tireless, and who wants to win at everything he does the way Greg does. Relentless is the word. He does a lot of listening and a lot of driving." As a leader, Takesue cites Greg's "energy and the way he handles people. He treats everyone the same. He treats a warehouse worker basically the same as he treats a senior vice president or CEO at other companies."

Jones knows what he wants in the people working *with*—not for—him. They need a double-edged work style, capable of working on a team and able to get things done on their own. They must be able to both hit and field, play offense and defense, lead and follow.

I think that my own strength is that I'm a good team guy. I've been able to find people to work with. And I think the other thing is that on the overall general management of the business, I've been able to help guide the business in the right way. But the most important thing I bring to the table is being able to bring all the right persons together. And I have to say it's not me, it's the team here that does the work.

We've learned that online companies are very fast paced and they're not for everybody. In recruiting people, you have to explain what it's going to be like to work in a high-pressure environment. Most people are not used to what I would call direct responsibility. Particularly in large companies, they are one off or two off the action. We hired a marketing person who was very high level at one of the big brands in the country. Yet, she was never really responsible for sales—she was peripherally responsible. She was in marketing and there was a separate sales group and yet another group involved in sales. In other words, she was removed from really getting results. She was responsible, but not really. If the sales didn't come in on target, it wasn't the end of the earth. There could be a hundred reasons. Here, if the sales don't come in, it's dead-on who has direct responsibility, something she wasn't used to. In the online world, people have to understand what kind of environment they're getting into. They'll be directly responsible because we're a small business. They have to be willing to do what it takes to get the job done. Unlike big company infrastructures, in our company of only 130 people and other small businesses, if the trash needs to be taken out, you take it out. That is not always an easy transition.

In building a thriving virtual auction house, uBid enables customers to review merchandise at an online storefront and place bids for products that are warehoused by uBid, ready for shipping within 24 hours for warehouse items. With its December 1997 online launch, uBid became a place for companies to sell excess merchandise: computer products (desktops, laptops, laser and ink jet printers, digital cameras), consumer electronics (CD changers, home theater systems, speaker systems, camcorders, phones, VCRs, TV/VCR combos), home and leisure products (kitchen, household, seasonal, personal care, outdoor appliances). Two and a half years after going online, 533,000 registered customers were making more than 2 million visits to the site per month. For them, it became bargain-hunting time. For investors, it was a stampede. Trading on the NASDAQ under the symbol *UBID,* a December 1998 $15 offering price for uBid soared to $200 per share within one month, becoming at that time the third most successful IPO in history.

As new as the Internet is, an old-fashioned attitude is the foundation of uBid—what the customer wants in product and price. Greg was not going to make the mistake of assuming what to put on the block or leave it to guesswork. Here is where his strong marketing background came to the fore. At APAC, he made his reputation by leading the way in signing up major new accounts (PacifiCorp, Boise Cascade, Farmers Insurance, Kmart). Before that, in the early '90s at Chicago-based Reliable Corporation, he was in charge of marketing, merchandising, operations, retail, and finance at the $200 million direct mail seller of office products. His marketing prowess stood out as he changed the direction of the company and increased sales by 18 percent and gross margin by 10 percent. In one year, his marketing plan turned around a company with multimillion-dollar losses into a profit maker. In starting uBid, first things came first.

We decided that we needed to find the value for the customer. So the first thing we did was to go around and survey the customers to ask, What would you buy online? *They came back and said that they wanted (no surprise) computers, consumer electronics, and sports equipment. So these products became our first three categories. That's how we started the business.*

We went to the manufacturers of these products and told them about this great idea for creating a market for their idle inventories—putting their products on the Web and selling them in an auction format. We'd take a cut off the top and the manufacturers would happily reduce their inventories. And the customers would be happy. At first, they, in effect, said, Sure kid, *and showed us the door. Things changed when I said that we would buy product because we believe that the idea is going to work. Then they said,* Maybe we can work something out, but we're not taking the risk. *So we started the business by buying a bunch of products and putting them up for bids. We developed a bunch of statistical models to make sure we wouldn't lose money, and we figured out how to move product so that we bought it, sold it, and still made money. We became an outlet mall online, one that uses an auction format rather than a fixed-priced format.*

The means of commerce, the choice of products, and the focus were all on target. The online boom was taking off and delivering customers, with Internet users projected to reach 135 million in the United States alone by the end of 2002. Well established as a communications medium and information resource, the Internet became a sales and distribution channel that was expanding rapidly. Moreover, all projections on products pinpointed computers and consumer electronics as the single largest retail category in the marketplace. From $2.4 billion in 1998 sales, forecasts targeted $9.6 billion by the year 2002 in the United States.

The match was just right. What customers wanted to buy vendors were eager to unload. Personal computers and consumer electronics products are characterized by quickly mounting inventories of closeout and refurbished merchandise that are the result of extremely short cycles and returned products. Refurbishing products adds yet another expense for vendors. Disposing of the excess has involved a labyrinth of inventory players—manufacturers, distributors, resellers, and retailers—and a variety of selling approaches that are handled almost as an afterthought. Selling is done through auction houses, catalogs, company stores or outlets, resellers and specialized retailers, as well as large superstores and mass merchants. Typically, the merchandise is handled as a supplementary product line or loss leader. What comes back to the vendor in revenues varies greatly and disappoints repeatedly. The liquidation process itself is the subject of tough negotiations, depending on quality, age, and condition of the merchandise. In the hands of a liquidator, the return can be as low as ten cents on the dollar. As an added drawback, these additional sales channels may end up competing with a vendor's more profitable, primary sales channels.

Given this environment, Greg Jones positions the uBid *idea* as a win-win opportunity. It provides a sales format that leverages the interactive nature of the Internet and reaches a nationwide audience. Vendors benefit from an efficient and economic channel for disposing of excess merchandise, including odd lots of closeouts and refurbished goods. Fast and frequent movement of products into the auction channel enables manufacturers to reduce their inventories quickly and minimize price erosion. Meanwhile, their primary distribution channels are not threatened. The response of vendors can be measured in the number who have signed on with uBid to unload inventory—from a starting place of zero and initial resistance to more than 600 signing up in two years.

uBid arrives at management's door with a compelling sales mantra—"Just Say 'No' to Idle Inventory." Instead of letting excess and refurbished merchandise depreciate in the warehouse, sell it fast, and earn maximum market value. Do so at a level unmatched by other liquidation and auction services. As for speed, uBid reports that typically it makes decisions on taking over inventory by telephone and submits purchase orders the same day. As to size of inventory, uBid will move one item or a freighter full and is ready to handle every step of the process, from refurbishing, warehousing, and payment processing to shipping and customer support.

Looking back, Tim Takesue recalls the first auction, which amounted to only $9,000 in revenue. "We basically started with one auction and now we've reached the point where we're running hundreds of auctions." Large companies liked the uBid idea, but hesitated because of all the paperwork and administration needed to conduct transactions for a limited number of items. Takesue credits Greg with overcoming the resistance with a revenue-sharing arrangement whereby the merchandise is consigned to uBid. Once sold, uBid receives a commission and turns over the rest of the revenue to the provider. "In an auction, everything sells," Takesue points out. "The question is at what price."

In the bidding process, uBid uses a counterintuitive strategy. It turns out that low opening bids attract more bidders and tend to produce higher prices in the end. The more bidding the greater the sense of involvement as bidders follow the progress of an auction and the greater their sense of empowerment. From the very beginning, uBid's customer sensitivity became the basis for success:

getting customers to keep coming back. Quality assurance is built in. Every piece of merchandise is checked on the way into uBid's warehouse. The "rule of thumb" is summarized by Greg: "No matter what the product is, if you wouldn't want to have it in your house, don't accept it. If you wouldn't be happy buying it, I don't care what it is. Don't accept it." On a second front, uBid has a policy of trying to keep bidding within bounds. It posts a "maximum price," with the built-in message, "Don't bid over this." Jones attitude is that "you don't ever want a situation where people are paying more than they should." If they do, they've been forewarned.

Meanwhile, Jones pays particular attention to two key features of uBid's business model: flexibility and variety in the buying and selling, all in real time. That includes the time span of auctions, which can range from one hour to weeks. To guide the variations, uBid's statistical models rely on projections that take into account traffic coming into the site, the number of actual bids, the capacity of its computing systems, the type of merchandise, the price points of merchandisers and other online auctions, and track records of items previously auctioned off. In comparison with today's precision and projections, uBid's early auctions were what Takesue depicts as an "adventure—a big adventure."

For starters, buyers have traditional bidding. On a typical day, they can bid by clicking onto an image of a Toshiba laptop, a ViewSonic monitor, an IBM Netfinity 5500, a JVC camcorder, D.G. Jewellery 14-carat earrings, or a Toshiba DVD player—all starting at $9. Or choose from Today's Top 10 Specials with a same-day closing that include computers, a projection TV, a home cinema system, a package of six golf shirts, an insulated nylon jacket, or a set of Tommy Armour 845s Steel Firm Irons. They, too, open at $9, except for the home cinema system which opens at $7.

The bidding adventure is only starting for the buyer, with links ranging from Antiques to Travel & Tickets. In between the choices include Beanies, toys and other collectibles, furniture, housewares, computer products, clothing, autos, real estate, and jewelry. Then there's Other Cool Stuff listed in columns showing lot number, description, quantity, current bid, closing date, and time (Pacific Time). This link is full of surprises: a Chinese Dadao fighting sword, a cigar cutter and torch, a three-foot-long blowgun, phones shaped as hot dogs, tomatoes and apples, sets of five Frosty Mugs, a hot pursuit New Jersey police car.

In its short span, uBid has put in place variations that customize the bidding to the participants and capitalize on the flexibility, speed, and scope of the Internet. Buyers can watch live on the uBid web site or opt for e-mail notification when they are outbid. They can use the BidButler feature, which follows the action and keeps their bid in play until the price goes over their limit. Straight sales—uBuy— also are offered with products in a lot offered at a set price, sold on a first-come, first-served basis. For good measure there are "Dutch" auctions in which lots start at a set price and decrease by set amounts as the buying continues until the lots are sold out.

On their part, sellers have choices on how to eliminate idle inventories. They can leave the auction to uBid and ship products directly to the winning bidder. They can process payments and handle customer support or let uBid do it. If sellers prefer, they can turn over their excess inventory to uBid to handle all warehousing, transactions, customer payment processing, shipping, customer support, and marketing. Products are auctioned off and shipped, with the seller paid a percentage. In other situations, uBid buys excess inventory at a fixed price and auctions it off. In a variation, uBid runs auctions on a web page that resembles a company's own page, creating an auction site that looks like the company's own.

Added features strengthen uBid's vendor appeal. When bidders make a buy, they're offered related products from the seller. When sellers need a fast infusion of cash, uBid offers payment options as fast as 10 days. uBid can handle everything, depending on client needs, including order and payment processing, warehousing, customer support, shipping, refurbishing, and extended warranties. uBid's message is its core competency: "From soup to nuts, we quickly resolve your surplus inventory needs."

Greg (Class of 1992, J.L. Kellogg Graduate School of Management, Northwestern University) has developed his own report card on what makes a successful online company, and he puts his own company—successfully—to the test. Three factors are "most important."

> *The first factor is an Internet company's growth rate. Is the company growing? If you see stalled growth, there's something going on there—either the competition has made inroads or something's not right internally. So I think growth rate is very important. I think quarter to quarter you'd better grow 10 percent to 20 percent. Ten percent at least. The second thing is repeat rates. In other words, how many people are coming back. I think that's critical to any e-commerce success. The other factor that's important is customer acquisition. How expensive is it to get people to try your web site. If you look at the successful e-commerce companies, it's inexpensive for them to acquire customers. In our case, we spend most of our acquisition money online with banner advertising on other sites. Bringing new registrants to the file is very inexpensive.*
>
> *What's important is focusing on the customer experience, making sure that the customer is taken care of.*

We like to look at the number of new users coming onto our site and into the auction business. Traffic and our registered users are important. I also feel that revenue growth and repeat business are the key metrics. If we're serving our customers well, our repeat rate should be substantial and we want to continue to build the business off the repeat rate. In our case, the repeat rate of 72 percent is unbelievable.

At uBid, the numbers are in tune with the high-flying Internet. Second-quarter revenues of $45.6 million in 1999 increased 33 percent over the first quarter and 575 percent over the same quarter in 1998. Registered users increased 41 percent to more than 533,000 from the previous quarter and 793 percent over the same quarter in 1988. Meanwhile, revenues soared in the first half of 1999 to $79.9 million—an 805 percent growth over the same period in 1998. In all, an auctioneer's dream as the average number of daily visitors to the web site reached 90,000.

As a hands-on leader, Jones's business approach is part paranoia, but in larger part a continuous assessment of opportunities in the online world and a proactive response. Paranoia fuels a first-mover strategy that produces an ongoing series of first moves.

We continue to move forward on our business plan and exploit every opportunity possible. So far, so good. The thing that you need to know is all guys like me live with paranoia. We are paranoid that something is going to happen, that we aren't doing enough, that we aren't working hard enough. We're afraid we're going to miss something, miss an opportunity. One of my responsibilities is to network and understand what's going on. I also rely on our people and the market to help us understand what's going on and what's hot out there and what isn't hot. So we have a new business group that's always looking to invest or find opportunities. We're very open to ideas, concepts, and suggestions. We listen to anyone who is interested in doing anything that they think is exciting. What we do is take our experience and mold suggestions into something that makes sense, even if the original idea isn't quite right.

Jones—listener, innovator, and initiator—keeps extending his auction formula, signing up new players to play the same auction game. He cites "several major strategic initiatives to expand our product offerings into the business-to-business and international auction markets by leveraging our technology, brand name, and customer base." What emerges is a demonstration of how online entrepreneurs identify, recognize, and respond to opportunities. The nonstop process cascades upon the market at the speed of the Internet. Under Jones's leadership, all of the following opportunities bear the same label and apply the same mechanism: uBid.

- *Auction Community*—Suppliers, once they are approved, can place products directly for auction on the uBid site. When the products are sold, uBid processes a credit card transaction and receives a commission, with suppliers doing the shipping to customers. It's another example of a win-win situation. Suppliers, who typically don't have the scale and technology to set up and run an auction site, benefit from uBid's infrastructure and gain access to its web site visitors (which reached 5 million visits a month when the Auction Community was announced in March 1999). In noting that the demand for access "significantly exceeded our original expectations," Greg cites its importance: "Now, through this major initiative, suppliers of any size can use uBid as an online auction gateway. This expands the number of vendors and products on our site."

- *Jewelry*—In an arrangement with D.G. Jewellery Canada, a leading high-quality manufacturer, uBid added rings, earrings, bracelets, watches, and loose stones to its live online auction. For D.G. Jewellery, according to its chair and CEO, Jack Berkovits, the "milestone partnership" opens up his product line to "millions of potential new customers." Greg identifies it as uBid's response to consumer demand for a "wider variety of products."
- *Software*—As the first online auction site to offer downloadable software, uBid partnered with Digital River, the leading provider in electronic software delivery. Digital River manages the delivery while uBid manages the transaction. Jones identifies the trend toward digital delivery of software as yet another important uBid opportunity.

On the business-to-business front, Jones has led uBid in new directions. A sign of the future is an alliance with Cahners, the largest business-to-business magazine company in the United States with 6.5 million readers and 128 market-leading magazines. The alliance started with Cahners subscribers in the printing, packaging, food service, and paper conversion industries. The subscribers are potential buyers and sellers in huge markets. Annual U.S. sales just for used printing presses, bindery, and converting equipment is estimated at $4 billion and at $160 billion overall for the printing and converting industries. Greg cites another "significant opportunity" for uBid—"to become a leading online auction solution for industrial equipment and to expand our presence in the business-to-business market."

In the same direction, uBid allied itself with Surplus Record, Inc., the world's largest directory of used and surplus machinery and equipment, to provide industrial manufacturers with real-time electronic bidding. The offerings range from air compressors, grinders, lathes, and presses to crushers, motors, and turbines. Surplus Record brings to the alliance worldwide circulation and 1,000 suppliers who use its web site for classified ads. uBid provides its brand name, online auction expertise, and infrastructure as an alternative to costly live public auctions, which typically incur a variety of overhead expenses. If held on-site, they can disrupt a company's operations, as well. Most significant, online auctions don't require bidders to spend time and money traveling to the auction site, with no guarantee of getting what they need at the price they're willing to pay.

Inevitably, uBid has added an international dimension by setting up a licensing agreement with an Australian media company, LibertyOne. uBid provides its software and brand name in exchange for a licensing fee and royalty from online auction sales in Australia and New Zealand. The arrangement includes an option to expand into various Southeast Asian markets.

In all this pursuit of opportunities, Jones's leadership of uBid matches his self-image. For him there's "no question" that he's an entrepreneur. Running uBid is more mission than management and marketing. Work is the way he defines himself. No philosophical theorizing about his role or about making a lot of money. His is the voice of the entrepreneur whose playing field is the marketplace.

> *You really have to be dedicated. Entrepreneurs are very hard workers, and it's hard for us to separate our business life from our real life. The difference is that the entrepreneur does what he's doing because he wants to and loves it. A business executive does his*

job because he has to if he wants to hold his position. The hardest part in running a business is making sure you take time for the family, and I have just a wonderful partner, my wife, which is the only way I can do what I do. I work six days a week, 18 hours a day and I work on Sundays as well. There's no substitute for hard work. In my case, I'm in the office by 7:00 to get a head start on e-mail and phone calls. I usually have meetings scheduled all day from 8:30 till 4:00 or 5:00—an hour apart. Probably every other day I meet with one of the executive staff. And on Tuesdays we have our big staff meeting. We have planning meetings after 5:00 at night probably till 9:00 involving 8 to 10 key people.

In Greg's experience, the Internet world is different from the traditional world of corporate work. And it's a big difference.

One thing in particular makes the online world different and that is the speed at which things move—10 times, even 100 times faster than in traditional large organizations. Big retailers or big companies getting into an online business have very little chance of being successful unless they let their online business unit go on its own. There's so much change and so much going on in the online world that you have to move quickly. In a big company, just to get a single contract through can take 60 days. In our world, you can do a multi-million-dollar deal in a week. The speed is unprecedented.

In all the moves Greg makes, the *paranoia factor* is at play as he looks at the brief, but very crowded history of the Internet's roaring nineties. No arguing with the survival of the fittest, but he takes particular note of how the profiles of survivors change.

Nineteen ninety-five and 1996 are what I call the tech years of online when anyone going online was a techie. Nineteen ninety-seven and 1998 were the years of the venture capitalists, and a little bit into 1999, where you ha[d] a lot of companies emerging [that were] supported by venture capital or, as in our case, by capital from a parent company. I think that next we're going to have the years of the big boys trying to get a piece of this Internet world, major traditional companies like General Motors, IBM, and Wal-Mart. Companies that are based on technology combined with business have the advantage in the marketplace. In the online world, which is much more crowded for sure, there will be a lot more companies and few survivors. Internet companies that started in the last couple of years know their space better than anybody and will survive, as will the big boys.

Two issues will make the difference in the long run, particularly for online businesses: better information and better service. Meanwhile, what it takes to be a successful entrepreneur won't change—to have a very exciting business that is high growth. That's where most successful entrepreneurs are coming from. As to the Internet auction boom, we're only in the second inning.

6

RUSSELL C. HOROWITZ—GO2NET

"If You Can't Build It, Buy It"

6

RUSSELL C. HOROWITZ—GO2NET

"If You Can't Build It, Buy It"

At a strategic point in a meeting between mighty
Hasbro and the hyperactive Internet company, Go2Net,
a mystified vice chair turned to an aide and asked
how the David-and-Goliath meeting was arranged. The
giant of the toy and gaming world, whose army of
games includes Monopoly, Clue, Risk, and Battleship,
was discussing a deal to get on the Internet with
an exuberant, curly-haired 33-year-old entrepreneur.
Traditional bricks was doing business with upstart
clicks.

The response on how they got together came in what
must have been an aide's tremulous voice, "He cold-
called us."

Go2Net's chair and CEO Russell (Russ) C. Horowitz
had been looking down the road to where the Internet
was headed and saw higher and higher levels of entertainment, particularly with online games. "Everyone
plays games," Russ reasoned at a time when online
gaming was getting scant attention. "What games
do they play? They play Monopoly, Scrabble, Risk,

Diplomacy, Clue. We have the technology for putting them on the Internet." Next question: Who owns the brands?

The answer was obvious: Hasbro, whose chair and CEO, Alan G. Hassenfeld, points out that his company owns 65 to 70 percent of the games people think of—"probably the most formidable library ever created in gaming." Russ was commuting from Seattle to Hasbro Interactive headquarters in Beverly, Massachusetts, to make a deal that combined Hasbro's branded content with Go2Net technology. Opportunity was knocking and Russ wanted to describe what was on the other side of the door as the number of online players multiplied. By the end of 1999, their numbers reached 38 million, particularly males between their teen years and their thirties. By 2002, industry watchers projected annual revenues of half a billion dollars.

Russ was working on yet another deal for his company, which was not yet three years old and already had a market capitalization of more than $2 billion. Hasbro would add another dimension to a network created by Russ and his high school friend, John Keister. Instead of TV stations, the network was being put together with branded web sites in the most promising categories—personal finance, search, commerce, and games.

For Russ, the art of the deal centers on a win-win outcome after talking and listening and putting together all the pieces, as in closing the Hasbro deal in December 1999 for a new site, Games.com, operated by Go2Net to deliver Hasbro games. Besides charging for some of the games, Hasbro would profit from selling ads and merchandise, while spending $60 million to create Internet versions of its games. Go2Net received $7.5 million to operate the gaming service, not to mention the increased visibility, prestige, and traffic for its network. As happens repeatedly, Russ's persistence paid off.

At the meeting when Hasbro's vice chair heard about the cold call, he couldn't believe how it all started. When I first contacted Hasbro, Go2Net was, by most standards, a nobody that wanted to meet with the company and talk about the opportunities for online games. We reached a point where I was meeting with all the top executives and directors from Hasbro. It was an 18-month process before we announced a comprehensive relationship in December 1999. As for me, once I think about something and it exists in my mind, my actions just follow. In my mind, I saw it. What do you do? You pick up the phone and call. It's that simple. And then you're tireless until it becomes a reality.

Unlike other overnight Internet successes, Go2Net exploded onto the Internet by acquiring, rather than creating, web sites. Russ's guiding principle is "If you can't build it, buy it." That's just what Go2Net has done since the company's start-up in 1996 when it was two people— Russ and John. "We were really the first company to say we're an aggregator and go out and do it," John says. "Now, there's a proliferation of companies that want to do business with us. At the same time, it has become much more competitive to get companies at a reasonable price and to find them before a competitor does. As an aggregator, we're going to go out and consolidate as many of these companies as we can."

The Go2Net partners added another entrepreneurial dimension, a first in the Internet boom, when they used stock in their company to acquire web sites. Acquiring rather than creating, buying with stock rather than with cash, going public rather than going all-out for venture capital, Russ and John spent only $6 million to jump-start a formidable Web network. Their acquisition strategy worked. In January 1998, Go2Net ranked number 77 among the most-visited Web destinations (as reported by the industry measurement firm, Media Metrix). Less than a year later, it was among the top 20, growing at five times the overall rate for the Web and at twice the rate of the Web's top 10 properties.

"Our original business plan," John recalls, "was developed with Russ running around the room waving his arms and talking, and me sitting at the table writing everything down in a manner that made sense. Russ had the vision. I wrote the business plan and walked it through, asking, 'How can we actually do this?' " The two guys in a room had already done plenty of homework, as spelled out by John.

> *We did a lot of research before starting this company. We got research reports from every investment bank out there, and we studied them thoroughly, some of them 100 pages long. We read through all the prospectuses on the companies that were going public at the time, like Yahoo!, Netscape, Infoseek, and tried to get some sense of where this industry was going to be five years down the line—meaning 2001, 2002. We saw that content would be the thing that people would focus on, whereas in 1996 people were focused on tools, browsers, and operating systems. We wanted to project into the future, since we wanted to be a winner in 2002 rather than in 1996. So we decided to get involved in the content game.*
>
> *When Russ says that we "raid garages," he refers to the kind of companies we were acquiring early in our existence. They were two- and three-person operations that wanted to be part of something bigger. We were able to identify technologies that were very sound, written by bright people who would fit into our organization. At that point, we did whatever we could to convince them that being part of something big was a better idea than remaining independent.*
>
> *We saw the industry itself as so disjointed that we*

could aggregate companies and create a network. That played into Russ's strength. If he gets in a room with a company that is interested in doing a deal with us, we'll get the deal done. And it will be on terms that are win-win. Clearly, we've done that time and time again, going up against much bigger and more storied companies than ours to get deals again. This was especially what happened early on as we came out the winner.

Back then in '96, there were a lot of doubters, certainly from the software industry and mainstream corporate America, who said that this Internet thing was just a flash in the pan. The same kinds of doubters are still out there, so you still need to be willing to embrace risk. I've got that willingness and Russ certainly has it. He's fearless. He was convinced that if we got in the game and were able to create a market position, no one would be able to beat us. That's what we talked about from early on. Let's get a market position, establish ourselves in two or three strong categories and from there we'll make sure that Wall Street and the media understand our story. We'll just outwork and outthink everybody else.

Go2Net's starting point was (and is) content. Russ and John reasoned that once Internet users choose a computer, a browser, and a home page, they need to decide on what they're going to access every day. Go2Net's answer is "sticky" content, what users want and what advertisers would pay for, advertising being one of the company's main sources of income. Russ and John went looking for the right content by analyzing what was on the Web. They set up a massive spreadsheet of the top 1,000 companies in 12 categories to identify the categories that were getting the most interest and looked as though they had the most staying power. That's how they chose personal finance, search, commerce, and games as the categories to focus on.

In the beginning, there was a hiccup when Russ and John amassed writers and editors to develop content for their November 1996 launch of sites. The sports site soon changed their mind. As good as it was, with basketball Hall of Famer Bill Russell and baseball great Joe Morgan as exclusive contributors, it cost too much and returned too little. Russ describes the moment of truth: "You have to be honest with what your resources are and what you can do." That's when the *buy-it-rather-than-build-it* policy kicked in as the partners searched for high-potential web sites that were just starting out and could be acquired as bargains. Less than five months after their launch, they took Go2Net public, so they could use company stock as currency to make acquisitions. John labels the profit side of the strategy as a "vending machine model," a portfolio of sites that are up and running with little overhead and little need for additional investment. Meanwhile, the sites produce revenue streams that have every potential to increase down the road.

As a business, Go2Net is a pure online play, possible only in cyberspace, never would have happened anywhere else, another online success story. But there's more. There's also a universal dimension that is typically a part of every entrepreneurial success. It's the part that resides in the personality and vision of the entrepreneur, the determined individual who's not technology bound but opportunity driven. As such, Russ Horowitz is a quintessential entrepreneur in action and personality, someone who "always had the feeling" that if he were dropped anywhere in the world, he would be successful, whether or not he knew the language. The vision part, as summed up by Russ, isn't complicated: "Being able to see things that either other people don't see or being able to see them before they do." For him, it begins with being a "learning junkie."

When something interests me, I have a desire to come up the learning curve as quickly as possible and that applies both personally and professionally. One of the things about me is that I don't really distinguish a lot between the two. As to the Internet, when I became aware of what was emerging and recognized what was happening, it was just like a lightbulb went on.

My particular skills and interests were an advantage. I had seen what happened in the PC emergence of the eighties and the ensuing revolution that added utility to PCs. Then I saw the network become the standard before the Internet become the next incremental step. I saw it all in a way that could mean something to me. It gave me a fairly unique foundation. So timing, in particular, was extremely fortunate.

Let me clarify what I saw. In late '95 and early '96, when people talked about the Internet, they really thought they were talking about one thing. They didn't distinguish whether it was the Internet as service provider or whether it provided software or browser, or whether it was a company that delivered e-commerce. It was viewed as all one thing. The first thing I saw was that the Internet represented a convergence of all sorts of different industries. In many respects it was a means to an end. Underlying the Internet there was a whole slew of individual opportunities that had their own dynamics and risks.

As best as I can remember, I was the first to talk about the Internet revolution as being similar to what happened in broadcast television. John Keister and I saw a lot of parallels to broadcast television and cable television. So early on, I developed a vision of where I thought there would be a real opportunity to build web sites. When cable came in, it wasn't the networks that thrived. It was targeted cable channels like CNN and MTV. The Internet is going to follow the same pattern.

So we decided, Let us [at Go2Net] be a niche player. *When I described it to people, they would say that it sounds like television or even magazines. I would say that the Internet has parts that are similar, but the Internet is its own thing. The challenge is not to be limited to what you're familiar with and what you understand—but to break the mold. In order to respond to opportunities, it takes certain individuals who aren't limited by the standard way of thinking. People talk about not seeing the forest for the trees. I think there are times when you really need to examine the trees on a micro level and see the details, and there are times where you really need to step back and really see the forest. The key isn't just the ability to do each of those. It's really the ability to do them at the right time.*

In "aggregating" sites to build a network, Russ doesn't lean on traditional yardsticks like earnings and revenues to identify companies as Go2Net prospects. He looks for high potential that can be reached at low cost, web sites "where the incremental cost of scaling up is minimal relative to the magnitude of the revenue opportunities." John, in his role as company president, adds his description of how Go2Net looks for, finds, and appeals to targets for aggregation.

There are a lot of companies in the categories we target, but not that many have the background to take their businesses and create value, whether that means finding a strategic partner to merge with or taking their own company public or even just keeping the books and running a profitable business. There are a lot of companies that have great technologists and great ideas, but don't understand how to run a sustainable business. After we identify leaders in different categories, we approach them and say, "Look, we've got a publicly traded stock. We're just getting started. You've got a great product. You can be part of something big. We've got great deal makers, technologists, and managers. Let's get together and build something." That's the approach we've taken and we've been able to get deals done in the categories that we feel have sustainable value.

Once a target for aggregation is identified, Russ swings into action with a "SWAT team mentality." Keister still marvels at Russ the deal maker. "He walks in, gives them the 'vision thing' and they sign on the dotted line. He has the ability to make other people passionate about being part of the team." When pursuing an acquisition, Russ is sensitive to the pride and passion of entrepreneurs who have created their own Internet companies. They didn't dream of pushing papers or clipping coupons. They are action seekers and frontline competitors to whom Russ presents a Go2Net offer that's been hard to refuse: "We basically give them the option to do the things they like and to give us the things they don't want to do." For Russ, it's a matter of mixing his predilection for mathematical thinking with sensitivity—"understanding people and what motivates them."

I take a mathematical approach to everything, math being something that I have really excelled in. I think about everything in terms of probabilities, like a calculus problem, with variables and unknowns. When I look at situations, I assess the probabilities of various events unfolding. If you identify two things that can happen, if one of them happens, then what? There are two more, and two more, and two more. After you mentally unfold this geometric sequence of possible scenarios, you go down a number of steps and figure out which one leads to an outcome that you think is good. You identify the variables that you need to bring about in succession to create that outcome. That's a place where I'm able to manage a lot of information, taking those things I know and using them to deal with the unknowns. It's a fundamental skill and if you combine it with the variable of understanding people, then you're in a position that can lead to the most compelling negotiation and sales. This is an area where I feel that I have done well and it's led to good negotiations and ultimately to decent results

The thing that I particularly don't do is fake what I say. You've gotta be sincere, and this inevitably creates credibility and makes you an effective salesperson and negotiator. In meeting with builders of companies, I don't tell them that I'm out to convince them to be part of Go2Net. What I set out to do is understand the management of the other company and help them understand Go2Net so that they have all the information they need. I don't try to get people to do something they don't want to do. I want to make sure both of us are committed to invest the time to work through the process and to get at all the relevant information so we make the best decision we can.

Russ is a deal maker who may even advise against signing up with Go2Net, as he did when discussing the company's first major acquisition with the developers of the celebrated search engine, MetaCrawler. Oren Etzioni, a computer science professor at the University of Washington, along with a colleague, had developed the search engine, which became so popular that it was causing a logjam on the university's computer system. By querying the databases of multiple Web sources like Yahoo!, Lycos, and Infoseek, MetaCrawler was coming up with the best results available.

As word got out about the search engine, offers to license MetaCrawler poured in and Etzioni was trying to figure out which one to accept when a mutual friend suggested that he talk to Russ. They met, talked, and, to Etzioni's surprise, Russ said that he'd love to have MetaCrawler on board, but suggested that Etzioni accept one of the other offers on the table because it was a better deal than he could offer at the time. That didn't happen. The Russ Horowitz effect kicked in. In February 1977, Etzioni made a deal with Go2Net and he has explained why. "What I found is that he's just a fantastic businessman. I was looking for a company that was well run, could achieve profitability, and spot trends." In 1999, Etzioni went further. He quit his teaching post to become Go2Net's chief technology officer.

In another Horowitz coup, Go2Net acquired Silicon Investor, the premier web site for financial discussion and a leading web site in number of paid subscribers. It was the prototypical "garage start-up"—two brothers, one woman running the site, 75,000 paid subscribers and much too much for three people to handle. So two and a half years after going online Jeff and Brad Dryer went to Silicon Valley in the spring of 1998 for a series of meetings and presentations with companies wooing them. Well-established companies with deep pockets, such as CNET, made their bids and then there was Russ, the underdog that the bidders and the financial press were ignoring. The competing offers were on the table when Russ and the Dryer brothers began meeting and talking for hours.

Russ laid out the "vision thing." He told the Dryers that if they wanted to sell out, more power to them. They had earned every right to do so. But then there was the Go2Net option. They could keep on running what they had started and keep their brand recognition, while working inside a larger organization that would mind the store and handle the corporate details.

Russ calls founders of web sites the "passionate" ones. When they sit at the conference table across from him, they surely recognize mirror images of themselves, particularly his SWAT-team style. Theirs is not the world of committees that deliberate and delay decisions, of reports that complicate negotiations, of teams that look for what's wrong or missing, of executives who are uncomfortable with uncertainty. When online entrepreneurs get together, they're in fast company. Comparing their style of operating with that of traditional bricks-and-mortar companies is like comparing a motorcycle ride with a bicycle trip. Russ, in particular, stands out as a fast mover, both in finding target companies and closing the deal:

> MetaCrawler—the Web's number one metasearch service, launched June 1955, acquired February 1997
>
> PlaySite—premier Java-based multiplayer game site, launched September 1996, acquired July 1997
>
> SiliconInvestor—the Web's premier site for financial discussion and information, launched August 1995, acquired June 1998
>
> HyperMart—leading provider of free services for business hosting, launched November 1997, acquired August 1998
>
> 100hot—index of ratings for top web sites in a range of categories, launched May 1995, acquired December 1998

John Keister, who's worked side by side with Russ as Go2Net has aggregated and expanded, still marvels at the mental processes and the drive of someone he describes as "the best CEO on the Internet," someone who "thinks long term, but also acts with urgency when it's necessary."

> *Russ is tireless. He's always been a competitor, always been looking for bigger and bigger challenges. He loves to read mysteries, to solve problems whether they're real or fictional. When we got into this business in '96, what he appreciated more than anything else*

was that we could blaze our own trail and set policy for the way we do business. The possibilities were only as limited as your mind and that leveled the playing field. That gave us a big leg up on companies with all that venture capital funding and on all the people with 10 to 20 years of background in the software industry who weren't ready for such a playing field.

As a CEO, Russ cares about every detail of what we're doing and it's not easy to find CEOs like that. There are a lot of smart people out there, but how many of them are willing to work seven days a week all year long and work 14- to 16-hour days or more when it's necessary? Russ has pulled many an all-nighter, and he will do whatever it takes to get the right deal done. That's the thing that Russ has and that he has instilled in all of our managers. It's a sense of urgency that sets us apart.

For Russ, his "most valuable time" is spent sitting back, thinking, and analyzing—as typically is possible on his many plane rides. These are the times free of meetings, e-mail, and phones, open-ended times, but not times in which he can stop thinking about business issues. "I can sort through, without interruption, my thoughts, which unfold like a chain of events in my mind. Since we started Go2Net, some of the best opportunities have come out of thought processes during those very times."

Then there's the action-packed Russ Horowitz, as succinctly described by Brad Dryer of Silicon Investor. "His energy and vision keep Go2Net going full blast ahead at all times. Sometimes we think he's not human."

Brad has a point and it goes way back. At 13, Russ read both bulging volumes and all three sections of the *Value Line Investment Survey*, which tracks, rates, and assesses all the stocks on all the exchanges. At 16 he ran his first 26.2-mile marathon. His prep school economics teacher, Bruce Bailey, calls Russ "the smartest guy I ever taught." (He backed up his judgment with a $2,400 Go2Net start-up investment that soared to $70,000 in three years.) Appropriately, the graduating class at the Seattle school, Lakeside, elected Russ most likely to succeed (the same school that Microsoft founders Bill Gates and Paul Allen attended). While in high school, he benefited from two experiences that he credits with developing people sensitivities that he brings to bear in negotiating deals—waiting on tables at the Seattle racetrack and selling shoes at Nordstrom.

When Russ enrolled at Columbia University to study economics, he faced up to an extra-added challenge from his Brooklyn-born father, a Yale Law School graduate practicing law in Seattle. Russ, his older brother, and his sister were told, "If you want something, you have to work for it and you've got to make sacrifices." For Russ, that meant paying his own way through college. While at Columbia, he worked as a security guard and four nights a week he unloaded trucks in New York's flower district from 11 P.M. until 3 A.M. To save on the cost of college, he obtained special permission to take twice the normal course load in his junior year so that he could finish in three instead of four years.

Russ was surely made for the high-speed, hard-work world of Internet start-ups where the track is always fast. To his father's pay-your-way challenge, he adds a favorite maxim from Nietzsche—"Only through pain comes knowledge." In his case, it means working "hard, efficiently, and consistently."

> *I always had high expectations for myself, always comparing myself to people who were much more advanced. When I came out of school and I was in my early 20s, I felt like such a failure that I hadn't accom-*

plished what somebody in his 50s accomplished. In many ways, I wasn't fair to myself. I started working at Lehman Brothers and Oppenheimer and was a senior vice president when I was 22 years old. So I was advancing quickly, motivated by a fear of failure.

Many people come to me and say, "Russ, we always knew that you would be successful." I step back and say, "Pardon my French, but that's bull." If you work as hard as I do and as efficiently and as consistently and then you don't have comparable success, then complain.

After graduating from Columbia in 1988 and heading to Wall Street where the action was, he began building his portfolio of knowledge, know-how, and experience. At Lehman Brothers and Oppenheimer & Company, he gained a reputation for developing and advising start-ups. As cofounder of the Active Apparel Group in 1992, he served as chief financial officer (CFO) until the company went public in 1994. He subsequently founded and served as general partner of Xanthus Capital, L.P., a merchant banking limited partnership focused on emerging technology companies and special situations. Before that, he "probably couldn't have even spelled Internet," but he could recognize opportunity in the exploding high-tech industry. He began contacting various West Coast start-ups and offering to come on board as CFO and help them raise money, but the right situation never materialized.

All the while, Russ and John had stayed in touch in a friendship stretching back to their high school days when they played together on the school soccer team, parted ways to go to college, and got back together in New York to share an apartment. In those two years living together as roommates, they started to talk about working together as business partners. When both moved back to Seattle, they reached a point where they wrote a business plan for a coffee retailing company. Then there was what Russ calls the "starting gun," the success of the Yahoo! and Netscape IPOs that triggered their Internet homework and team-work. Their business partnership parallels their soccer-playing days, Russ as center forward, John as goalie. Russ scoring, John holding the fort. John speaks both for Russ and himself in describing how the partnership has worked out—the way partnerships should.

> *It's been a very good relationship because from the outset we understood where our areas of influence would be, what our strengths are, and how we would build the company. I was very comfortable with the idea that Russ was going to handle the Wall Street end of things and that he was going to be the primary point of contact on the deals we do. I knew he had a lot of strength in those areas. On the other hand, he knew that I had the background to manage operations and to build a team that would be a consistent one, that would have a good attitude supported by incen-tives, and that could deliver on the products and the promises that we made to the partners.*
>
> *From the beginning we felt that we had the right core principles in place to have a good partnership. And it's still working out very well today. We still are pretty much in the same areas of influence as when we started the company. One thing that really helped us was that we've known each other for 20 years and we've already had the fights and the highs and lows that many people don't have until they start work-ing together. We already understood each other's strengths and weaknesses and pressure points. In working together, we make sure that we take care of our issues behind closed doors. We put them on the table and are honest with each other. If we need to*

scream and yell, we'll do that, but we always walk away happy with the conclusion.

On the financial front, they've worked out a relationship whereby Russ receives a salary of only $36,000, while John (after a raise) receives twice as much, but still only $72,000. Of course, their personal wealth has soared thanks to stock holdings in Go2Net, with Russ owning the larger share of stocks and options. At the end of 1999, John's approximate 2.5 percent share was worth $87 million, Russ's 10 percent was worth $348 million.

Their salaries signal a low-key style in the Internet world of skyrocketing market values. "Burn rate"—the amount by which company spending each month exceeds revenues—is not the direction they want to travel. As Russ has assured his stockholders, Go2Net is sticking to "fundamental business principles: Control overhead, spend money as you make it, and work diligently at creating shareholder values." Of the $15 million the company raised when it went public, $9 million was still unspent in March 1999 when Microsoft cofounder Paul Allen concluded a $426 million investment deal that made him Go2Net's biggest shareholder.

When that happened, online watchers, analysts, and investors were no longer ignoring what Russ and John had put together and were continually expanding. They already had emerged as a unique start-up that was in the black with significant revenues from online advertising (more than 300 clients). Other revenues come from more than 100,000 subscribers of Silicon Investor and from licensing Go2Net technology to other Internet companies.

Meanwhile, their acquisition trail is paved with success and soaring values. MetaCrawler, the top-rated search engine, was brought on board for a mere $100,000 and a percentage of gross royalties. Russ estimates that Hyper-

Mart, which was bought for $4 million, is worth hundreds of millions.

Go2Net's headquarters at the Wells Fargo Building overlooking downtown Seattle, Puget Sound, and Mount Rainier was luxury leased at a bargain price. Even Russ was surprised to pull it off. When Go2Net was looking for a larger office space, he heard that First Interstate Bank was going to vacate its 47th-floor perch after being taken over by Wells Fargo. The floor-to-ceiling windows, panoramic views, plush carpets, and designer furnishings added up to a pricey setup that looked beyond the range of thrift-conscious Go2Net. "The broker wasn't even going to show us the space," recalls Russ, who made an offer within his tight budget figuring the broker could only say no. Instead, the broker, who was eager to lease the space, said yes and included $300,000 worth of designer furnishings in the deal. Russ ended up paying less than half of Seattle's going rate of $40-plus per square foot.

From one deal to the next, Russ's successes at Go2Net have broadened his view of goals. Each time he reached one it was no longer meaningful. He set another. Then the dawning:

> *I can sincerely say that by the time I reached a level where I could say to myself that I am a success on some level, I'm not sure that I cared as much as I expected. I was asked not long ago what I thought was my greatest accomplishment. I'd say now what I said then. I don't think I've done anything great. I think I've done a lot of things that were good. So I think I'm successful, but it doesn't put me on a pedestal. I'm doing a good job. I've applied in this industry the skills that apparently I have. I've used my ability to process many, many variables in rapid succession. I couldn't have a better environment and a better industry for someone like me.*
>
> *That's why I characterize this as being my time.*

KEN PASTERNAK—
KNIGHT TRADING GROUP

"Figure Things Out and Build a Business"

7

KEN PASTERNAK—
KNIGHT TRADING GROUP

"Figure Things Out and Build a Business"

Ken Pasternak started early, very early.

As a first grader he sold candy to his classmates at a profit.

As a schoolboy he sold his new bicycle, bought at wholesale by his father, at retail—then developed a thriving business in used bicycles by the age of 12.

As a college student he bought cars in Canada at bargain-basement prices and sold them in the United States for profitable markups. By the time he graduated from college, rather than owe money on student loans, he had money in the bank.

As a stock trader, he went from a $175-a-week beginner to the director of trading at the premier market maker on Wall Street earning an annual salary well over $2 million.

By 1995, he was cofounder of Knight Trading Group (formerly Knight/Trimark), which made a profit from day one with stock orders that originated on the Internet. Within four years, Knight is number one in that arena, while overall it executes 10 percent of all U.S. stock exchange share volume. The trade publication, *Equities,* summed up Knight's "phenomenal growth" as "unprecedented." *Fortune* added its tribute, reporting that "almost overnight [it] has muscled its way into one of the most competitive industries in the world" and calling Knight "the backbone of the online trading revolution." The Jersey City–based company quickly became the envy of Wall Street, executing more NASDAQ over-the-counter retail trades than Merrill Lynch, Goldman Sachs, Salomon Smith Barney, and Morgan Stanley Dean Witter combined.

Ken set up Knight around an innovative idea that appealed to online order-entry and small regional brokerage firms. Ken offered them the opportunity to own part of a partnership that would pool their individual retail orders into one giant stream of orders. Ken set out to provide these retail orders with what large institutional investors had access to—a single point of entry to buy and sell stocks. And he succeeded, leveling the playing field for smaller players by giving them the wallop of high-volume institutional buyers and institutional sellers in getting the best possible price.

On one hand, he is a traditional entrepreneur with one foot in the past—in the historic activity of trading, of getting the best trade executions for Knight's clients in the give-and-take art of buying and selling.

On the other hand, he has seen the future created by technology and the Internet for individual self-directed investors wishing to buy and sell stocks. He has gone out and created a channel where tomorrow's empowered investor can go today to receive the same speed, low cost and dependability in their securities transactions long enjoyed by institutional investors.

His starting point was what he identified as the "value proposition" of the Internet. It is a breathtakingly fast electronic enabler for trading stocks and an unprecedented information medium. "It is not only a mechanism to deliver orders to and execute transactions in the marketplace, but it is also a medium to obtain information and analyze it." Ken focused on two factors—volume and volatility. Volume drives revenues in the process of buying and selling stocks. Volatility drives profits by enabling traders to take advantage of changing prices, the more ups and downs, the more opportunities to profit from the shifts.

Ken is sticking to his lifelong entrepreneurial formula. "I've always been a person who has liked to figure things out and build a business around it. If that's the quintessential entrepreneur, then I qualify." The venue has varied, but not the underlying formula.

> *I've been described as someone with one foot in the past and one foot in the future. I certainly didn't invent a new activity. I took a traditional activity—market making—and applied a futuristic viewpoint to that activity. It involved understanding how the Internet and technology are changing all the rules of the game. I started by understanding the rules of the game and then built a business model that could flourish under those rules and respond quickly to change.*

Even with his childhood candy business, Ken recognized opportunities that others missed. His upstate elementary school didn't let its students, who were bused from a wide surrounding area, go home for lunch. But Ken could go home because he lived "right around the corner," as his 81-year-old father, Heinz Pasternak, recalls. "Ken started being an entrepreneur when he was 6 or 7 years old. On his lunch hour, he went down to the local grocery store and bought penny candy and sold it for a nickel to the other schoolkids. Being an entrepreneur was in his blood."

His father brings up the bicycle episode as an example of Ken's marketplace mentality.

When my three kids were small, I was able to buy three bicycles at wholesale. Each one got a bicycle. Kenny turned around and sold his bicycle and came back with what was then considered a lot of money. My older son and my daughter asked him where he got the money and he said, "I sold my bicycle."

So the other kids asked Kenny, "Can you sell our bicycles?" (Which he proceeded to do.)

Ken reciprocates with a recollection of his father's influence.

My father's enthusiasm for entrepreneurship is unceasing. He has had at least five to ten different entrepreneurial endeavors during my lifetime. From buying real estate to various enterprises associated with the automotive industry—selling used cars, a gas station, a towing business. In his late seventies, he started a car service because he was bored. Even to this day, he remains an entrepreneur. Just the other day he wanted to buy a house with me for resale. I guess I got the entrepreneurial disease from him. I learned from his mistakes and I learned from some of his successes.

A paternal enterprise led to Ken's collegiate used car business. While Ken was attending the State University of New York in New Paltz, his father, back home in the small upstate New York town of Fleischmanns, was buying and selling used cars. He had a deal with a local new car dealer. Because Heinz would buy the dealer's entire inventory of used cars, he got a special price. Heinz could then put a low price tag on the cars to move them out the door.

One day, when Ken was home from college, he asked how much his father wanted for a Volkswagen parked in the corner of the used car lot. His father said $800 and

Ken said, "I want to take that car to college. I'll give you the $800 the next time I come home from school." Once on campus, Ken sold the car for $1,400 to a fellow student. What he did was no different from what he has mastered in the stock market: trading and making a profit on price discrepancies. On Wall Street the rules are far more complicated, but in essence it's arbitrage, whether in bubble gum, bicycles, or 18,500 different U.S. stocks. "My whole life has been about pricing inefficiencies," he says.

The Volkswagen was only a beginning. As Heinz reports, "Ken's not easily satisfied. Period." Ken discovered Canada as a source of car bargains. With a partner, he began bringing in run-down cars from Canada where he bought them for very little and then fixed them up. Soon his brother and sister, his cousins, and his partner were going with him to Canada to drive bargain-bought cars across the border straight to a repair shop. Once repaired, Ken sold the cars at dealer auctions for $2,000 or more for cars that cost less than $1,000, repairs included.

After graduating in 1977 with a degree in education, Ken's first stop was not the classroom but selling for Dictaphone, where he was predictably successful but far from satisfied. After six months at Dictaphone, he was sitting in the office of a vice president of Troster Singer, a division of Spear, Leeds & Kellogg and, at the time, Wall Street's number one market maker. Ken was there because he wanted to trade stocks. The vice president offered Ken $175 a week, which he promptly accepted, though it was much less than he was earning at Dictaphone. (By moonlighting, he also earned $100 a night tending bar.) After three months, the vice president called in Ken and gave him the chance to trade his portfolio while he went on vacation. Expectations were low: He didn't need to make money as long as he didn't lose any. Ken did much better. When the vice president came back from vacation, Ken's trading skills had generated $200,000 in profits, more than 20 times Ken's annual salary.

Ken's next stop was the CEO's office where he announced that he wanted to become a trader for Troster Singer, which was *the* place to be a stock trader. When the CEO pointed out that there were people in the company who still hadn't made trader after 10 years, Ken wasn't fazed. He let the CEO know that he had mastered the trading business and could readily get a job elsewhere. The president got the message, and promptly put Ken to the test. His first trading assignment was the company "dogs," the stocks no one else wanted to struggle with.

The outcome was predictable for a trader with a talent for "understanding all the rules of the game" and a young man "not easily satisfied." If trading is compared to horse racing, it was like giving an unproven jockey a series of long shots to ride. Ken finished in the money in his first year. By 1987, he was a special limited partner at Spear, Leeds & Kellogg, a manager in the trading room, and creator of one of Wall Street's first training programs. By 1991, he "ran the room" as director of all the firm's trading operations. In an 8-year span, his division's net profit increased from $20 million to $65 million.

It was then a wonderful self-centered world for traders—until the early 1990s and the beginning of the Internet explosion. A trader-friendly marketplace thrived on minimal competition while providing little value for investors, for whom market makers were invisible. Investors called stockbrokers or sent messages to online brokers' computers. Orders then went to market makers who posted the buy or sell price through a network of computers, often using their own capital (liquidity) to conclude the sale. What they had to buy to complete a sale, they held in inventory while seeking another investor.

Traders were lion kings in the Wall Street jungle—
dubbed "the rock stars of the business world" by *Fortune*
magazine. They made money in a protected habitat. They
operated differently from the specialists at trading posts
in the New York Stock Exchange (NYSE), where buy and
sell orders were executed in an auction market. In the
over-the-counter world, prices were determined by a
select group of dealers who bought and sold stocks out of
their own inventory, if necessary. They could maintain
wide spreads between the prices they were willing to buy
or sell a security, while passing along the costs to
investors.

At Troster Singer, Ken was riding high and working
closely with Walter F. Raquet, who joined the firm in 1992
as head of marketing and technology. The turning point
that led to the creation of Knight was a clear case of
entrepreneurial synergy between the two of them.

> *Walter and I were working on a five-to-ten-year busi-
> ness plan for Troster Singer when we started to have
> an interesting kind of percolation between the two of
> us. Where I was very knowledgeable about what was
> happening at the point of sale, Walter was very
> knowledgeable about what was happening at the
> strategic level with CEOs and other decision makers.
> We were two people with very complementary and
> unique points of view: tremendous strength at the
> CEO strategic level and in trading methodologies.*
>
> *Walter knew there were a lot of small brokerage
> firms that wanted to be in market making. I knew
> from the business model that individually they
> weren't big enough. Also, none of them knew anything
> about market making. We worked together over the
> course of thirty days to create a business model. In
> the first stage we were thinking of doing a joint ven-
> ture with a single player.*

I was thinking about the logistics, which necessitated tremendous scale. Walter was thinking about the capitalization structure. He's the kind of guy who cuts to the chase and he had a eureka. "If Ameritrade, E*TRADE and Waterhouse aren't big enough alone to partner with, then a group of them are big enough. Let's get a group of them together." Walter went home one night and did some math. Then he called me at home to say that he thought he could get seven of these firms to invest in a joint venture and then I said, "Yes, that'll most likely work." (As it turned out, 27 broker/dealer firms came on board as founding investors in Knight.)

As we developed this plan, we started to understand the implications of what was going to happen in the business. A next-generation market-making model would have to be done in a totally entrepreneurial laboratory as opposed to the status quo corporate structure. It was revolutionary. It involved the whole concept of equitizing a large body of order entry firms on behalf of self-directed individual investors. No other market-making firm has done that before or since.

When Ken told his father about his decision to leave Troster Singer to form a new company, he heard a response familiar to other high-flying company executives who quit to start a business. "You're crazy!" His father, who had always made a living but never made it big as an entrepreneur, heard his son announce that he was leaving a job where he earned more than $2 million a year. Why leave all that behind and take a big risk? "Well, Dad," Ken said to his father, "there are a lot of things you don't understand." Needless to say, Heinz, who wasn't alone in failing to grasp Internet opportunities, doesn't hesitate to admit how "right" his son was.

Ken's trading know-how and Walter's contacts and knowledge of brokerage companies moved the project ahead to its high-speed, high-volume operation. What was crucial was mastery of the mechanics of Ken's business model—superior client service, industry-leading technology, large-scale, highly sophisticated trading methodologies, and an experienced entrepreneurial-minded workforce of traders. For Ken's traders, that means dealing in information on stock inventories traveling at the speed of nanoseconds and in processing 700 orders per second.

Ken recalls a meeting with the head of a German stock market: "He was bragging about how good his system was. It had handled 150,000 trades on a recent day. We do 300,000 trades on a slow day!" For the four quarters of 1999, average daily trades of 405,000 were executed for clients. In fact, Knight executed 90.7 million trades and traded 81 billion shares in 1999, which ranked Knight second behind NASDAQ and the NYSE and fifth largest in share volume worldwide.

What technology made possible, changes in rules and regulations made inevitable. Ken points to the drop in retail commissions to $5, technology that automated the trading process, and players like Knight that revolutionized it—all of which Ken worked through in setting up his company.

> *To begin with, the first rule was to create a culture that was client focused and added value on the level of executing transactions. No one was doing that. The second rule was that technology was going from a necessary evil as viewed in the early nineties by technophobic CEOs in the trading business to a tool to create tremendous competitive advantage across your whole business model. The third rule was that you had to be a skilled trader or the margins were going to get you.*

Before 1994, every single market maker in the United States made a lot of money. The bad ones made 20 percent on revenues and the good ones made 50 percent. So it was a business where there was no margin pressure anywhere. That changed when 80 percent of the revenue potential of market making disappeared. From an average revenue capture of $50 a trade, it went to less than $10 a trade. The only way to survive is by using technology, by automating everything with unbelievable amounts of volume. The fourth differentiator was trading methodologies.

In making a market, we went from operating on a trade-by-trade basis to what is known in the business as a "proactive liquidity guarantee basis" (to use capital, when a particular stock is not in inventory, to go into the marketplace and buy enough of it to fill an order). *Because everything's automated, we give guarantees all the time for almost every stock. We have a portfolio of approximately 18,500 stocks and our clients determine the size, the price and the point in time they want their trades executed. You must have a very complex trading methodology that creates enough positive revenue streams to make a living from that trading.*

It's a constantly changing process. What worked three months ago doesn't work anymore. We have proprietary algorithms for evaluating information around order flow and inventory management to produce profitability. How we do it is proprietary, as is the way we manage information at the desktop. Keep in mind that investors and all other kinds of traders can see the same information that we see. The marketplace is getting smarter and smarter. Our comparative advantage is our proprietary trading methodology, our superior processing technology, and scale.

We have a lot of smart people here, Ph.D.s, people

with degrees in mathematics and physics. We are constantly trying to create a comparative edge in how we use trading methodology and technology to optimize the trading process. We see ourselves as thinking the way the proverbial kid in the garage thought, as having the same kind of innovative element in our company. We're continuously looking through the front windshield at what's ahead of us and are always cognizant of people who are developing new technology processes that might become part of the marketplace. Keep in mind that buyers and sellers are meeting within our systems to the tune of about 400 million shares a day. We have connectivity to almost anyone who has an account with an online order entry or regional broker/dealer.

At Knight, three parts make up the whole for more than 950 employees. Knight Securities makes markets in stocks listed on the NASDAQ and the OTC Bulletin Board of the National Association of Securities Dealers (NASD). Knight Capital Markets (formerly Trimark Securities) trades New York Stock Exchange (NYSE) and American Stock Exchange (AMEX) stocks over the counter (the Third Market). Knight Financial Products (formerly Arbitrade) is an options market maker on the Chicago Board of Options Exchange (CBOE), AMEX, and the Philadelphia Stock Exchange. In an environment where the action is electronic and a "smart building" is important, Knight avoids the high rents of New York by setting up headquarters in Jersey City across the river. "We're positioned near New York, the capital of securities trading," Ken says, "but we pay just $18 a square foot on an annual basis."

Ken the traditional trader has become the futurist entrepreneur who wrestles with the way the Internet and technology "have changed the rules of the game." Where Ken once operated "very intuitively," he now outlines a broad-based mural of the entrepreneur and fills in the spaces with specifics.

Being an entrepreneur is a lot more complicated than being a trader. I started with a very simplistic understanding of trading, which has been around for centuries. You buy low and sell high. Essentially, in the used car business I was arbitraging market inefficiencies between various auctions. Entrepreneurship involves putting together all the elements of institutionalizing a business model that has competitive advantage—which I wasn't doing when I was in the car business. I was doing a little bit of that when I was a corporate operative at Troster Singer.

Here at Knight there are probably 20 or 30 elements in running a business. Some of them revolve around the big idea but a lot of them revolve around understanding the rules of the game and delivering a comparative advantage for clients across all the key determinants of success. And I think that's what entrepreneurship is about. First off, it's understanding the big idea. That's maybe 1 percent. Understanding the rules of the game may be 9 percent. The other 90 percent is all about implementation skills and execution.

With us, the main idea was that technology was going to change the balance of power from the institutional side of the stock market to the individual self-directed investor and that when you create a consortium with equity firms, you create scale. It meant using technology to leverage everything. The next part was to understand that the marketplace was moving from a nonclient service, noncompetitive arena to a client-focused, highly competitive arena. We had to understand that we were a client service company that had to add value for clients. By the way, that wasn't a reality in the market-making business before 1994.

What happened "in the business" after 1994 has borne out what Ken saw coming. As with all first movers, the trends he saw are obvious in retrospect. But his initiative was "revolutionary" when he moved ahead. For Ken Pasternak, the highly favorable outlook for online trading encompassed demographics, buying patterns, technology, and statistical projections (matched against actual numbers). His reasoning is a road map of the way the mind of an online entrepreneur turns information into an idea that works.

• Three "powerful" trends were increasing the participation of self-directed individual investors in stock investments. In growing numbers, individuals have been taking control over the management of much of their assets in planning for retirement. The Internet has created an information explosion that supports and promotes such empowerment. And their numbers increase as more and more baby boomers retire and live longer in an aging America. Every eight seconds, another American turns 50. In the first decade of the millennium, the number of over-50 Americans will increase by 45 to 60 million, a segment of the population that is heavily invested in stocks and has the most time and inclination to handle its own investments. By the end of 2002, online trading accounts are expected to leap to 24 million, six times as many as the 4 million in 1999. Ken views this "self-directed individual investor revolution" as providing "tremendous growth opportunities" for Knight. He cites what has already happened. Knight started 1999 projecting 500,000 transactions as its daily maximum for the year. Instead, early in the year, the company had to raise that processing capacity to over 1.5 million trades.

• As Americans accumulate more money, they will invest more. As people of all ages and backgrounds become comfortable with the Internet, they will use it more and more to trade stocks. Once individuals get online, their propensity to trade stocks increases fivefold, according to Forrester Research projections. Ken has identified "a secular trend toward more and more individual online trading."

• The more open the Internet becomes as an information source, the more it will be used by online investors. Practically every professional investment service is already providing market data in Internet packages that are free. Ken calls this "added value" on the Internet that enables investors to find a match for their investment profiles, manage portfolios on their PCs, and trade in a totally automated fashion. All of this he identifies as a stimulus for online trading. "My guess is that as the popularity and comfort level of using the Internet for various e-commerce activities increases, you will see people of all kinds of trading behaviors embrace it."

Down the road, Ken sees a future where "every stock in the United States will trade on what you might call a virtual exchange with the Internet as its backbone." It's already happening. In a July 26, 1999, report on electronic trading called "Wall Street Revolution," *Barron's* cited an update from an expert on stock markets, Benn Steil of the Council on Foreign Relations in New York: "All natural economic distinctions between stock exchanges and broker-dealers have broken down. Exchanges and brokers are now doing exactly the same thing."

Ken singles out the difference that his venture makes. "We believe that we provide optimal executions and proactive liquidity to the marketplace. If we did not exist, the client would receive inferior trade executions at much higher costs. After Knight's IPO in July 1998 at $14.50 a share, investors added their endorsement as the company's stock soared beyond $80 in the ups and downs of

NASDAQ trading. At the end of 1999, the stock closed at $46.00, with Ken owning 7.2 million shares.

At Knight, trading can take place in approximately 18,500 different U.S. securities, from IBM on the New York Stock Exchange to Microsoft on the NASDAQ to small cap stocks to bulletin stocks to "pink sheets" (daily over-the-counter security quotes) to American depositary receipts (ADRs). The process is automated end to end, with the majority of orders executed within five seconds. The company has more than $450 million in equity capital, enabling the company to commit up to $1 billion if appropriate—capital available for its traders so they can buy or sell stocks for inventory in order to maintain a fair and orderly market.

Inside Knight, traders work in teams that are managed by a senior market maker and operate with an emphasis on interaction and exchange of information and know-how. While trades are executed in a high-speed, automated process, decisions on buying and holding stocks for inventory are made by the company's traders—a distinctively entrepreneurial feature.

Ken describes the trader's mentality (which personifies his approach) and the system at Knight (which he set up). Even a brief look makes it clear that this particular online enterprise is only for the *very* knowledgeable.

> *As a trader, you're going to make evaluations about the direction of price so you can benefit from its direction. Think of it simplistically. One of three things is going to happen whenever anybody sells you a stock—it's going to go up, it's going to go down, or it's going to stay the same. About 95 percent of the time the market changes. The real question is: For that 95 percent of the time, can you identify which are favorable opportunities to trade and which are unfavor-*

able? Liquidate when it's unfavorable and maximize the favorable ones. You're doing over billions of dollars worth of transactions, hundreds of thousands of trades, millions of shares a day. Keep in mind that the positive revenue capture here is less than a penny. It's all about scale.

We watch all of our trading. Imagine a giant spreadsheet—in real time—totally customizable in over 240 fields of data in a matching process. It's like the military. The trading room manager is like a general. There are colonels, captains, lieutenants, assistant team captains, master sergeants. Then you have the market makers, they're the lieutenants. Everybody's in the chain of command, everybody at every level can watch what's happening across this intelligence spreadsheet and localize information to their area of responsibility in real time. All the market makers and all the team captains and trading room managers are under very strict capital risk guidelines—one of the reasons why Knight's number of trading loss days are negligible in the history of our five years.

Ken singles out Knight's traders as the company's front line, sometimes described as "350 Kenny Pasternaks." He personally recruited and hired the first contingent of 80 from the elite group of Wall Street's top traders. The offer they couldn't refuse wasn't money, considering how much they earned, including hefty bonuses. It was opportunity and challenge in the form of performance-based compensation, leading-edge technology, and massive amounts of order flow, leadership in trading methodologies, and— later—stock options. "Keep in mind," Ken points out, "these are all performance-based employees. They can have a significant upside." They are also future minded in responding to Ken's reputation as a very savvy player who understands technology and has a handle on what lies ahead in the evolution of the marketplace. They came on board because they had an entrepreneurial mentality and because they responded to the Ken Pasternak message.

> *You're going to make a bet even if you stay where you are. Or you can leave and come here. The securities industry is at a crossroads. You have to make a decision on where order flow is going and where your career is going. It's probably easier to stay where you are as a kind of nondecision, but in a way, it's a bet in itself.*
>
> *Many of them made the decision to stay where they were. But the others made the same decision as Walter and I, the ones who really understood where the business was going. Walter and I said that we could stay where we were and make $3 million or more a year or take advantage of an opportunity to do something that's more exciting and create something.*

Entrepreneurial achievers pass Ken's "risk-it-all, let-the-company-be-your-life test." A favorite example of someone who failed the test was the managing partner from a major brokerage firm who was "ready" to join Knight to run its European operation for a $15 million bonus, a $1 million base salary, a nine-to-five schedule, and a generous vacation package. He had come to the wrong company, as Ken promptly points out. "His idea of being an entrepreneur was to get paid like he was a senior management executive at a major Wall Street firm and still own part of the upside."

Instead of freedom from risk, Ken's focus is on delivering results—for himself, his staffers, and the company. He means business.

> *There's certainly a personal style that I have here with both my fellow managers and employees. Part of it goes to who I am—a lower-middle-class type of guy who created a lot of success for himself. I believe there's a very strong commitment on my part and this company's part to operate as a meritocracy and to encourage all of our employees to be very entrepreneurial. There's a very flat line of management here and a lot of direct access to my office. I think you'll find that most of the employees here identify with me and operate in a very entrepreneurial way. Quite differently than they do in many other companies.*

In a self-directed assessment, Ken identifies himself as basically a businessman with an eye on his legacy.

> *It's like being an artist or a professional athlete or an entertainer. That's what you do, that's who you are. I liken myself to an artist. If you're an artist, you paint. Picasso painted till he was 80, maybe even 90. If you're a businessman, you create business value. And that's what I do. It's as simple as that. And the public company canvas is the most exciting canvas you can paint on. If there's a legacy here or a penny at the end of the day when Ken Pasternak leaves, it would be that Knight would be one of the major financial services institutions in the United States and that it will be talked about in the same breath as Merrill Lynch and Goldman Sachs and Citicorp and General Electric.*

8

WILLIAM SCHRADER—PSINET

"Shaping the Internet—and the World"

WILLIAM SCHRADER—PSINET

"Shaping the Internet—and the World"

In 1989, the future "Father of the Commercial Internet" and his wife, Kathleen, held a family meeting with their three young sons, who knew as little about something that would become the Internet as did the venture capitalists and corporate executives their father, William (Bill) Schrader, was contacting. One after another, he approached 30 venture capitalists and not one of them grasped what he was talking about, much less offered any capital. Nor did he make any headway when he called on corporate executives at technological giants like IBM and AT&T. As to technology experts, for the most part they viewed computer networking as mainly the domain of government and academia with only limited business applications. Bill remembers the initial dismissal of the Internet as "the tool of the academics and play toy of the government." It was certainly not viewed as a place of business, much less the future of business.

Bill envisioned a future with a network of computer networks—the Internet. He has identified it as "the neurological system for the global economy," the place where

businesses will have to go to do business. He was determined to start a company that would connect companies
to networks and enable them to take advantage of
unprecedented connectivity.

Back then in 1989, Bill was "a leader of the Internet
before we even knew what to call it," as the *Washington
Business Forward* pointed out 10 years later in one of the
many interviews that focused on the vision and the enterprise of Bill Schrader. When he decided to leave academe
and go commercial, Bill knew he was "right." It was the
explaining part that confounded him and confused his
listeners. "I was right. I knew I was right. It was just a
matter of learning how to explain it to people. It turned
out that I couldn't explain it to anybody so we just did it."

But before taking the plunge, there was the matter of a
family conference with three young sons who were still in
elementary school. He wanted them to know about the
all-or-nothing stakes and to get their support for what he
was going to do. He planned to put the family into hock to
start a company that would provide a service hardly anyone understood at the time. ("Maybe 50 people in the
world understood," he figures.) Bill wanted the boys to
know that their college tuition money was going to be put
on the line. He already had been discussing the enterprise with his wife, who provides a flashback on the family decision making behind what became PSINet, the
world's first and largest independent commercial Internet
service provider.

*Bill and I had been talking about going into business
for quite some time and we basically decided that's
what we wanted to do. I wasn't entirely sure what all
of it meant—but I knew what he was doing at the time
was a nonprofit regional network project. Bill said that
the Internet was definitely the future as far as business is concerned and that it would definitely be big.*

He also talked about what our personal wealth would be if we succeeded with the new company—although that certainly wasn't why he wanted to do it. Bill described to me various scenarios, which—if you look at his original business plan—have been pretty much all true down the line. It's been weird. It even happened along the same time schedule he predicted, though he did underestimate the amounts of money involved.

At the family meeting, we talked about using the money we were setting aside for college tuition and we told the boys that we'll either have the money for them to go to college—and lots of it—or we might have a problem with tuition. We asked them, "Where do you guys stand on that?" The boys were cool. They said, "Let's do it." I think if we had known everything that we would face when we started, it would have been much harder to go ahead. But naïveté was in our favor because we had no idea of what the obstacles would be in getting to where we are today.

For the Schrader start-up, in addition to the college funds, betting the bank meant getting a second mortgage on their house, selling their used car, and using Kathleen's credit cards to the hilt. (She had 18 unsolicited Visa and MasterCard accounts that provided $87,000 when charged to the maximum.) Add money from family and friends who "didn't understand a word of the business plan," but trusted Bill. Altogether, the start-up had $320,000 and 33 business customers.

In less than a decade, Bill was running a company with a market value in the billions and he could sum up (in PSINet's 1998 annual report) the ways in which he was delivering on his original business plan. "The Internet is reshaping the world and PSINet is shaping the Internet. Through vision, focus and timely execution, we have become much more than just an industry participant, we are truly a market leader. We are in the enviable position of helping to define and create one of the most dynamic industries in the world."

What has happened confirmed the Schrader vision. By the mid-1990s, the business Internet market was growing at an annual rate of 50 percent in the United States and projected to grow at 70 percent in the rest of the world. Projections for global sales on the World Wide Web set the outlook at $400 billion by the year 2002. As for Schrader, he has remained as outspoken and optimistic as ever about PSINet's prospects. Never more so than when he put AT&T on notice and shocked a CNBC TV interviewer by predicting that one day there will be no AT&T as it is known today.

Bill doesn't mince words. He says, without a shadow of doubt, "The entire physical plant of all telephone companies in the world is junk. Understand, junk. Do you know what that means, trillions of dollars. We can replace it all. In fact, we have. In the next four years, 80 percent of all voice traffic is going to be over the Internet." As giant killer, Schrader's business is connectivity for businesses of all kinds and sizes.

Phone companies are his favorite target. "The best thing they could do over the last 30 years is have call waiting on top of the dial tone." Bill argues that the present environment is not a telephone environment and therefore phone companies will not thrive. "They will die." As for PSINet, "We are not a telephone company. We are a replacement for the telephone company." He sees a near future in which the Internet will replace phone service in quality, performance, security, and cost, with long-distance calls at a flat rate. Phone calls will follow the e-mail model, costing virtually nothing.

He likes to use the dinosaur analogy, which is appropriate to someone who describes himself as a "Darwinian thinker." Ask dinosaurs, *Who's in charge?* he says, and without hesitation they will reply that they are. "We little mammals say 'right' and let them be. We're not going to tell them they're dying. We're the mammals, because we can adapt. We saw the meteor coming, we hid in a cave, all the dinosaurs croaked, we came out and said, 'Hey, looks pretty good.' The Internet is the meteor."

Bill's vision was born in academe where for five years he was in the middle of computer networking, the little-noticed parent of connectivity and the Internet. He was putting connectivity into action in a series of assignments that conventional wisdom in the 1980s regarded as no more revolutionary than adding call forwarding to a phone system. As executive director and cofounder of the Theory Center at Cornell University, he helped plan and build the $100 million supercomputer center to support basic research in computational science and engineering. As part of his work at the Center, he led the project that developed the NFSNET Backbone Network that amounted to a pilot for the Internet. The Network connected the national supercomputer centers and became the basis for the NSFNET system.

When Bill became founder, president, and CEO of NYSERNet, the first regional Internet network, he could see something much bigger on the horizon. At that point, he was providing networking services to university, cor-porate, and government users in New York state in a non-profit environment. One glaring clue to future demand was the eagerness of business executives to sign up and pay for the e-mail services of NYSERNet. Bill was sitting in his office at the New York Telephone Company, fielding the phone calls that became wake-up calls.

I was getting 8 to 10 phone calls a day from prospects who had read a newspaper article or heard about our network. They said to me, "We'd like to get connected to your network so that we can participate in this *thing called the Internet." The people who called came in two groups—one was companies, the other was a college or university. When a college or university employee called, they asked me how much we would pay them to connect to our network and how much money we would give them to train themselves to use our network. When the business people called, they asked how much they would have to pay me to get connected to our network. These calls hit a ratio of 10 to 1, 10 corporate to 1 university call, every day for six months. Understand, we charged $30,000 a year up front for a 56 kilobit connection to our network. So nine corporations would call up to ask if they could send me a check for $30,000 for one university person who asks me to pay them to connect to my network. What did I think? It's pretty damned obvious. So I went to my board of directors at NYSERNet and said, we should go commercial. It was a 100 percent academic board and they said no. So I said, I quit. And I did. I bought NYSERNet and formed PSINet.*

Bill took his stand against the academic view with its nonprofit orientation and the government approach with its penchant for regulation. It was a case of individual enterprise combined with personal ideology. He describes himself as an American libertarian who believes that the government "should do one thing—provide for national defense—and stop." He was convinced that it was time for free-market competition in the world of online connectivity.

I care about doing the right thing. I could see what the right thing was and I didn't want to see the government using its power, as it had for the last seven or eight decades, to support telephone company monopolies. I don't trust the government—never have—never will. I didn't like the fact that telephone companies had tremendous power and used that power willingly to abuse their customers. They would stop innovation—intentionally—because it would hurt their revenue streams and they would lock out their competition from using it as well. I thought that wasn't right. So I wanted to set up a system where nobody had any power to stop innovation. So I did.

He has a shorthand answer to the origins of his original and ongoing Internet vision: "Just thinking, I guess." He had direct experience with what networking could do and foresaw what that would mean for business. "I had always anticipated that this Internet thing should be part of the communications fabric of the world, not just in New York state." Companies would be able to get connected with all parts of their organization, their customers, and their supply lines. The connection could be direct, immediate, and global. "Disintermediation" was on the horizon, "the removal of everybody in the middle." This would move companies toward more extensive services, more complicated and extensive applications, more ambitious solutions. The demand for bandwidth and a supporting infrastructure would escalate. As far as Bill was concerned, all of this was "very easily predicted."

As a biologist, I might ask where did life form. Life formed not on land, not in the desert, not in the dirt, not in the ocean. It formed at the interconnection of water and land. That's where the action is. That action is always at the interconnection point. As for the Internet, the foundation is connectivity, but it's no longer the heart. The heart is the traffic in electronic commerce and the systems that enable it—the software, the services, the security, the computer systems. It's all enabled by something called connectivity.

As to PSINet's core competency:

> *Staying with customers and their requirements for the twenty-first-century e-commerce environment. That means to anticipate the design of reliable technology, to have the cash to acquire it, and to actually build a worldwide system that does it. Then care for that customer in the training and use of said services.*

Bill has been fighting conventional wisdom so long in pursuing his vision and its implications that he resorts to a standardized response to skeptics and naysayers, "I'm right. You're wrong." In doing so, he has run the risk of being stereotyped and of having the workings of his mind simplified and/or distorted. Fixating on that response is like characterizing Michael Jordan as an athlete who can slam-dunk a basketball. As a many-sided player in the Internet world, Bill operates at, and beyond, the cutting edge as innovator and entrepreneur. For a close look at his mental and visionary apparatus, there is his self-image for starters. His wife adds a perspective that goes back to their high school days and to her involvement in PSINet from its founding. For good measure, there are reactions from people who have observed him and have had dealings with him. What they say sheds light not only on him but also on the emerging breed of online entrepreneurs, arguably a breed apart.

As for Bill, he's a realist, free of both false pride and foolish modesty. He describes himself as a biologist (his college major at Cornell University), an entrepreneur, and a carpenter. Never a specialist.

> *I'm a generalist. So if you ask anybody what I'm really good at, the answer is nothing. If you ask anybody who really knows me about my expertise, the answer is nothing. I'm not an expert in anything that*

the world would view as a discipline. I am an entre-preneur. In fact, I'm probably the best entrepreneur I know because I'm willing to make a tough decision when I don't have all the facts—simply because time is of the essence.

My personal role in technology is translator. I listen carefully to people who know what they are doing and show them respect. People are willing to talk about what they do in life. They talk and I listen and learn. I can understand what a technologist is saying from the business side and then share that translation with the business people who can't understand the technology. And then learn more about the business and take that back to the technology people. The key is to create an environment where the technologists are respected by the business people and the busi-ness people are respected by the technologists.

I'm a smart guy, but I don't think I'm one of the smartest guys around. There are many, many, many smart people around. It just happened that I had a weird mix of upbringing and experiences. Also psy-chological flaws. I couldn't focus on one thing so I focused on a lot of things. Because I had never done anything very well, I could see certain things that other people didn't see.

He characterizes his personal odyssey as "following opportunity." At each twist and turn, he inserts "I got tired of . . ." He got tired of studying biology in college so he started a business doing remodeling and painting. Next came physics because it's like biology, then supercomputing "which was really physics." That turned into computer networking, which almost overnight became the Internet. The next and lasting opportunity came along when he decided that "it was time to go commercial."

As someone who knows Bill from their school days in Utica, New York, his wife Kathleen fills in the details of what Bill calls the "mix of upbringing and experiences" that shaped him. He grew up in a world of hard work, self-reliance, and modest means. His father made ends meet by working as a carpenter, with little to spare. As a youngster, Bill earned his spending money as soon as he could. Nothing special in that experience, but a sign to Kathleen of things to come—"a spirit that has always been entrepreneurial."

In elementary school, Bill started by selling Burpee seeds door-to-door and, as soon as he could get working papers, he found a part-time job at a drug store that opened near his home. While in high school, he became the store's assistant manager, was class treasurer all four years, and led a sales team for the senior yearbook that sold enough ads to turn money over to the school. In college, Kathleen and Bill teamed up to bake and sell cakes. They both became accomplished bakers by following recipes and practicing until they got it right, then they sent letters to the parents of students offering to deliver a cake on their sons' or daughters' birthdays. Their specialty was cheesecakes. As a married couple, their first joint project was rebuilding the house they bought. Once again, it involved learning what needed to be learned. All along the way, Kathleen has watched Bill in action.

> *There's something ticking around in Bill's head all the time. It's an ongoing process. He'll sit and think in his office or on the back porch, but most of the time he's thinking at the same time [that] he's doing something else. Doing e-mail, in the car, at dinner. When he says, "I'm right, you're wrong," it's impatience. He sees through the maze of things and he's thought things through, but is too impatient to discuss it down to the final details. He'll go through a multidimensional*

series of possibilities as in a giant three-dimensional chess game. Actually, Bill is a genuinely modest guy and that's one of the things that has made people underestimate him. But I'll tell you when the last man is left standing, I'd put my money on him.

One of the pieces that people don't see is that Bill is politically interested in leveling the playing field for the have-nots. He believes the free market can take care of things. If you rely on government to pay for things, sooner or later it takes over, telling you how you can use it, when you can use it, and for what purpose. Bill thinks it all should be open. We agree on that. Democracy should be grateful for entrepreneurs and the Internet. Look at the entrepreneurial effort on the Internet, things that people wouldn't have been able to start if they had to rely on established banks for capital, established newspapers for publicity. When we started out, people didn't understand the Internet. We had to spell it out one letter at a time and explain what it was. As we started to use it, we began realizing its potential.

A view of Bill from the consultant side is filled with intriguing superlatives. "He's a very nice, down-to-earth guy who's very enthusiastic . . . He's feisty, controversial, outspoken, brash, and an extraordinary visionary. There were a number of other people in that computer network connecting the schools in New York, but he was the one person who saw that it was going to be the wave of the future. He goes leaps and bounds beyond anyone's normal thought processes. When I heard him say that one day his company would basically replace AT&T, I believed that I [would] see the day that it happens."

The visionary who once had trouble getting anyone to take his Internet vision seriously now attracts the attention and scrutiny of Wall Street analysts, business writers, and savvy observers of the Internet. He has been described as developing "a reputation as a fast-acting, hard-talking businessman who's just as ready to push ahead with new business schemes as he is to abandon them." Other Schrader descriptions include "intense, fair-minded" . . . "For pure gusto, it's hard to beat the outspoken William Schrader." . . . "He has the sort of smile you might expect on a mysteriously rich uncle—bright but tidy, with easy switches from apparent gravity to apparent mirth." . . . "He doesn't play a lot of games. He can be very disarming" (from an executive who negotiated with him). . . . "He's very direct. I always knew where Bill stood" (a PSINet supplier). . . . "Known for his laser-beam focus on providing commercial Internet service, he is also considered intense, fair-minded." . . . "a pixyish character with a mind running at the speed of a Pentium processor" . . . "His vision can change abruptly, which is both a good and not such a good thing. He's not frozen in concrete. If he sets his mind to something, he can change if he sees opportunities. He tends to be very ambitious." . . . "never afraid to take intelligent risks if it would further the company's goals" . . . "The man is the company." . . . "He is the personification of an entrepreneur."

Bill relishes the entrepreneur label.

> *I am an entrepreneur. I'm probably the best entrepreneur I know because I am willing to make a tough decision when I don't have all the facts—simply because time is of the essence. For me, the most important thing is to look back and feel comfortable that I did the right thing, knowing what I knew at the time. When people don't know everything, that's when people decide not to decide. In our situation, that's a mistake. You have to do something. Sometimes it's a mistake, but at least you made a decision. Those who didn't make a decision are no longer run-*

ning a company. I always want to know that I did the best I could with what I had at the time, without being foolhardy or cowardly.

Moving ahead, changing course, growing through expansion and acquisition, he's never looked back since starting Performance Systems International (changed to PSINet in 1995, the year the company went public). Traveling fast the Internet way, a company that started with 15 employees and 40 commercial customers became in less than six years a full-service operation with 8,200 corporate customers, ranging from small businesses to Fortune 500 corporations. In a single year (1995), PSINet quadrupled its staff of 125 employees in specialties that ranged from technical support to marketing. The same year its Points-of-Presence (POP) increased from 150 to more than 240 on three continents. Bill reported his "strategy for success" to the company's newly arrived stockholders: building "the industry's most advanced network" and offering "a fully integrated array of products and services on a global scale."

Bill sharpened the company's focus by exiting the consumer market and selling his software subsidiary. Instead of providing Internet access to individual customers, he sold his consumer subscriber base to concentrate on business customers. PSINet was then in the position of carrying the traffic of consumer-based Internet service providers (ISPs) while avoiding the overhead of marketing, billing, and customer support. He learned a lesson and didn't hesitate to reverse course. "We got into it [consumer access] not understanding the complexity and the need for intense marketing efforts and customer support. We changed our strategy in 18 months because we were losing too much money, and it was a good thing to get out of."

Bill has an Internet view of reversing decisions and changing course. "The Internet is very tolerant of errors,

errors of judgment, errors of strategy, errors of execution. The Internet is very unforgiving of performance. If you don't perform, your customers leave." He cites PSINet's retention rate of corporations as a benchmark for the industry: increasing from 87 percent in 1995 to 94 percent in 1996. That was the year he added new services with PSI IntraNet, PSIWeb eCommerce, and PSINet InternetPaper (to send faxes). In 1998, less than 10 years after he couldn't get venture capitalists to listen to him, Bill raised over $1.1 billion in capital to carry on what he has called "an aggressive expansion program" to buy ISPs and network facilities. At the end of the 1990s, PSINet's nonstop growth reached 225 POPs in the United States as the major slice of 600 POPs in 25 countries and its customers included 25 percent of the Fortune 500. By then, from PSINet headquarters in the Washington, D.C. suburb of Herndon, chair and CEO Schrader was leading a company with 3,000 employees and 60,000 business customers. For good measure and for a price of more than $100 million, its name is emblazoned on the renamed home field of the National Football League's Baltimore Ravens— PSINet Stadium.

Bill's strategy calls for high-speed growth and then a flexible approach in bringing companies on board so that the fit become fitter in his Darwinian approach. He rounded out the company's first decade by continuing his signature style of merging vision and action. In a 20-month period, he acquired 50 small ISPs around the world, with every intention to keep on acquiring. That takes money and that's what was raised: at one point, $3 billion in debt and equity in 18 months. The next vision was to become an "Internet Super Carrier." The action part involves building global data centers (60 in three years, costing billions). His goal is to become the largest Internet supplier in the world's top 20 telecom markets and a major player in 50 countries (owning optic fiber and hosting centers).

We guard against entrepreneurs coming up behind us by a very clever tactic. We encourage them. When we see somebody eating our crumbs, we pour out more crumbs, and then we open up the back door and we let them into the kitchen. We let them eat all they want, and then we put them inside the company and we grow them as fast as we can.

Our strategy is to purchase fiber, build and own hosting centers, and buy and integrate companies. That is our strategy. I personally was involved in the first 10 acquisitions. Then we found people who were sensitive to the process that's required to do it successfully. They honed their skills and went from buying 10 in three quarters—to 10 in two quarters—to 10 in one quarter—to 10 in one month. There is now a full system to do this, run by individuals who are trusted by me and everyone in the management team. Now I don't even know that we're acquiring a company until I read the press release. I also trust them to know that it's okay if they make a mistake or two.

A decision at PSINet can be made in hours whereas in a large company it would take a lot of PowerPoint presentations and months. Here, it could be done in the hallway. For example, do we move $150 million to Japan to acquire 3 companies? Yes or no. We're ready to go. First of all, the decision usually would have been delegated to our Asia-Pacific leader. If for some reason it needed approval here, there are at least four people who could make the decision and wire the funds. Around the clock, our people are available no matter where they are.

We understand that time is of the essence. That drives everything. You have to question the notion of doing marketing studies. If you ask a market that has never seen a product what they would think of it, you'll always get the same answer. If time is of the essence and you know you can't get any more data, you have to go on your guts. On average, if you take 10 entrepreneurs, 2 or 3 might have a good gut. The rest probably are just out of sequence in time horizons. A different year, it would have worked.

As an entrepreneur, Bill acts—without apologizing. He calls his approach *persistence.* "It's doing what I know to be right and damning the torpedoes. I actually don't care what people think. I know what's right and I do it." There was the time, for example, that his board wanted to back off a major purchase of fiber to carry Web traffic when faced with a drop in PSINet's stock price to $4. No way, argued Bill. The board had thought the purchase was a good idea before the price drop. He told the board the change of mind was "stupid" and pushed through their approval. "So we did it," he reports, "and the stock went to $20. So was I a genius or just persistent?" (In its ups and downs, the stock soared to $73 in April 1999. Bill is convinced that it's a three-digit stock.)

Starting his work day at 7 A.M., sometimes earlier, riding a wave of 200 e-mails a day and a continuous flood of information from his staff, he remains the nonstop listener, learner, and doer. And always outspoken, including a comparison with the way online entrepreneurs operate against the way large bricks-and-mortar companies operate.

It's a different culture. We think time is of the essence, the others think money is of the essence. They think that by having $20 billion or $200 billion they can withstand us. We laugh at them because we can make a decision and implement it in the time it takes *for them to hear their own employees tell them the same thing that we just did. We can take an idea, decide, and execute on it—completely—in the same time it takes them to hear of the idea. It would take them 18 months and it would take us 18 days to complete the process. Speed and timing are what the Internet is all about. If you're willing to look at a situation and recognize the truth and deal with it, then you can deal with the Internet. It's a thing called knowing what you're doing.*

Bill, who is at the center of the action, will toss off a provocative remark about what he wants to do in life, "I still don't know what I want to do." In the next breath, he will describe himself as a "builder," something that's in the family.

I'm a builder. My father's a builder. My great-grandfathers before him were builders. The only thing that's different is what you're building and how much it costs. If you stop worrying about where the decimal point is, you just decide what makes sense and if you're not afraid of making decisions, then it's easy. It's not money. It's time—it's who you spend it with and what you do with it. A lot of people in the world think about money. I think of money as a tool.

When Bill revisits his view of the future, the Internet looms larger than in any of his previous projections. Instead of the Internet carrying 80 percent of voice traffic in four years, it becomes 95 percent in three years. Instead of 80 percent of commerce depending on the Internet in less than four years, it becomes 100 percent in less than three years. By that time, instead of 80 percent of all nations treating the Internet as a tax-free trade zone, it will be 100 percent. As to people who don't share his view of the future, he sees them as making the mistake of viewing "traditional values and traditional power as having some relevance to the future. . . . that's their error." More certain than ever that the Internet will change the world of business, he places himself in the middle of the action: "I want to change the world in my lifetime."

Pierre Omidyar—eBay

"Bring Power to the Individual"

9

PIERRE OMIDYAR—EBAY

"Bring Power to the Individual"

At dinner in a San Francisco Bay restaurant, a pony-tailed, 28-year-old software techie drifted into a conversation with his fiancée about, of all things, Pez candy dispensers and how hard it was for her to find collectors for trading them. From that exchange, a legend worthy of Silicon Valley has developed about the multi-billion-dollar phenomenon, eBay, the world's largest personal online trading community.

The legend is close enough to what happened, as adjusted by Pierre Omidyar to reflect his actual thinking process on the way to becoming one of the twentieth century's entrepreneurial tycoons (ending the century worth more than $5 billion as founder of a company with $20 billion in market value—more than Sears and JC Penney combined). He's the first to acknowledge how unpremeditated his success has been.

I really started eBay not as a company, but as a hobby. It wasn't really until I was nine months into it that I realized I was making more money from my hobby than my day job. One of the things I always wanted to do on the Web was bring power to the individual, ordinary people like me. The other thing occurred when my wife, Pam—then my fiancée—was talking about how difficult it was to find fellow collectors in the Bay area for trading Pez dispensers. The two ideas came together.

Being a software engineer by training, I was interested in doing interesting things and learning about new tools. That's how I got onto the Web. It was to help myself learn more about how it works. I also wanted to create an environment where individuals could benefit from the Internet. The businesses that were trying to come onto the Internet were trying to use the Internet to sell products to people—basically, the more people, the more stuff that could be sold. Coming from a democratic, libertarian point of view, I didn't think that was such a great idea, having corporations just cram more products down people's throats. I really wanted to give the individual the power to be a producer as well.

So looking back, trading Pez dispensers was one of the factors I had in mind when I created eBay. It wasn't that specific, having the conversation about Pez dispensers and then the next thing designing a web site. I got a general idea from the dinner conversation and grew the idea into creating a marketplace. So I originally developed a dozen categories of things, such as automotive, computer hardware, computer software. Originally, the web site wasn't specifically focused on Pez. It was focused on creating a marketplace between individuals. I had been on the Internet since my college days and I was really attracted by the efficient market idea. We could bring people from all over the world together in one place and trade in an efficient market, and thereby they derive direct benefits by participating in that marketplace.

Adam Smith's "invisible hand" had, in effect, come to the Internet wearing a glove fashioned by an idealistic techie. In a global auction marketplace, both seller and buyer can reach for fair market value based on supply and demand without time-and-space limits. Anyone and everyone in the world can do business. An auction with global reach gives sellers the best possible chance to get a good price and a fair profit while giving buyers control over what they pay in pursuit of what they want. Anywhere becomes somewhere, anyone can become someone who buys and sells. The marketplace of individual buyers and sellers rules and reigns, without interference from the enabler.

Adam Smith's *Wealth of Nations* was reappearing, appropriately, in entrepreneur-dominated Silicon Valley. As Smith stated: "Every individual intends only his own gain, and he is in this, as in so many other cases, led by an invisible hand to promote an end which was no part of his intention." Or as a writer for the high-tech magazine, *Wired,* reported in describing how he got hooked: "eBay is a cross between a swap meet in cyberspace and a country auction with computer-driven proxy bidding. The auctioneer is one of eBay's servers." The *Economist* pronounced the online auction phenomenon "one of the most valuable innovations wrought by the Internet."

Online auctions constitute a New Age marketplace where buyers and sellers trust each other—just as enlightened participatory management was also built on trust, in that case involving customers. Pierre is a great believer in trusting the customer. "I'm very proud of the fact that eBay has shown it to be true that 99 percent of the people are honest and trustworthy. My premise has held true. Otherwise, eBay would not be trading $10 million a day between members."

Pierre also found that eBay has brought collectors in a nation of collectors out of hiding and enabled them to participate in a community of fellow collectors. Validation and participation are powerful driving forces. Often, when Pierre talks to collectors, he finds that their wives and friends "don't understand their passion for collecting a particular object. . . . Now that we've hooked them up with a whole community of people who have the same passion, they feel validated." These communities know no boundaries, such as the nationwide Doll Chatters who meet every week to compare notes and share collecting expertise on a chat board that's become their "hometown."

With the Internet as enabler, eBay started in the cyberspace equivalent of a log cabin, Pierre's home office, then moved to the living room of an old friend who became his start-up partner, Jeff Skoll. Pierre Omidyar recalls his thoughts in the early days after eBay boomed from its Labor Day launch in 1995. "I remember saying that if we went in the beginning to venture capitalists or to business analysts and told them about the kind of business we were starting, they would have laughed at us." Jeff adds his recollection of a meeting the same year of a Commerce Net group, filled with techies who were at the cutting edge of the Internet. The moderator asked the 300 people at the meeting for a show of hands from those who had actually bought or sold anything on the Internet. Only three hands went up from the likeliest group of Internet customers, including Jeff who had bought a compact disc.

Soon, Pierre and Jeff realized that trust was supporting a powerful marketplace phenomenon—auction fever. The trust dimension, in particular, was contradicting conventional wisdom. When the eBay concept was presented to a business school meeting, the reaction was predictable: *People are going to rip each other off.* Pierre and Jeff were confident that this wouldn't happen. Because they turned out to be right, reality vindicated their vision. The overwhelming majority of sellers care about their reputations, and they constitute a powerful self-regulating, self-controlling force.

In less than five years, eBay was putting 350,000 new items up for auction every day in more than 2,900 categories—from china to chintz chairs, from teddy bears to trains, from furniture to figurines. The continuously growing list of 2,900 categories includes collectibles, antiques, memorabilia, trading cards, toys, dolls, coins, stamps, books and magazines, jewelry and gemstones. By the end of 1999, eBay had listed more than 126 million auctions, with more than 60 millions items changing hands.

eBay's 10 million registered users made it the most popular site on the Internet in terms of total user minutes (according to the Media Metrix June 1999 Web report). More than 1.5 billion page visits a month were flooding in and they were not click-and-run visits. Whereas each visitor to the widely popular Amazon site was spending an average of 13 minutes a month at the site, eBay visitors average 1.75 hours. eBay emerged as the giant among online auctions whose sales as a whole totaled $4.5 billion in 1999. The projection for 2002 is $19 billion, according to the Forrester Group 1999 Online Auctions Report. As eBay continues to go up and up and 'round and 'round in the new world of the Internet, Pierre sees trust as the built-in, sustaining monitor that all village communities—global villages included—share.

> *On the surface, it may look like we're just a place where people bid, buy, and sell: an auction site. But underneath it all, it's really a very complex web of trusting relationships that people—buyers and sellers—have built with one another so that they can actually do business. Our core competency is under-*

standing and serving that community of buyers and sellers.

On eBay, it shows up in our feedback form. We encourage people to give feedback to one another. People are concerned about their own reputations, and they are very easily able to evaluate other people's reputations. So it turns out that people kind of behave more like real people and less like strangers. They develop a close relationship after sharing their interests around a collectible—whether it's antique automobiles or Pez dispensers. [His wife has built her Pez collection to more than 400 dispensers.]

Not only does eBay facilitate feedback with our own chat rooms, but people develop their own mailing lists and they talk to one another by e-mail. It's something you can't actually see on the site unless you participate in a transaction yourself. So we have created communities that are built around a common area of interest, which is a very, very key part of what we do.

[To foster community] the only thing you can do is have a set of values. The customer's experience is not under our direct control, whereas in every other business it is basically under the company's control. A company creates the products, the selling places, and the brand, and trains the sales people. But in our business, the customer experience is based on how users interact with each other. While we can't control them, we can have a certain set of values that we really believe in and encourage our community of registered users to adopt. That's why from the very beginning I have told our own people that most people out there are basically honest and good and want to do the right thing. Sometimes, people have disagreements, but it doesn't mean that they're mean, dishonest, nasty people. You can deal with those disagreements and you can still do business with

them. You should treat people the way you want to be treated yourself.

It was very critical from the beginning that we understood and believed in those values internally. They're so important, so fundamental. If it was only kind of a public relations game or sales pitch, people would sense it. So it's been really critical that everyone in our company understand that we had the same culture internally as we did in our community externally.

All this comes from a realization that behind the bits and bytes and e-mail addresses there are real people like you and me. In eBay's world, not only are they people like us, but they also share our interests. They're very enthusiastic about antique cars or fine arts, and so you can develop a personal relationship with somebody that you've never met.

To emphasize eBay's "community values," Pierre has made an official declaration of attitudes and expectations for buyers and sellers. Inside the company and among the company's fans, the values are dubbed "eBaysian."

"We believe people are basically good.

"We believe everyone has something to contribute.

"We believe that an honest, open environment can bring out the best in people.

"We recognize and respect everyone as a unique individual.

"We encourage you to treat others the way you want to be treated."

Looking back to his childhood, Pierre traces eBay's founding culture to his mother's influence: "My mother always taught me to treat other people the way I want to be treated and to have respect for other people." As far as he's concerned, these are "good basic values to have in a crowded world."

Is it working?

eBay's answer is a powerful statistic: As of July 1999, bad transactions amounted to only ⅓₀₀ of 1 percent.

eBay relationships are liable to continue off-line. Users have planned vacations together, chipped in and bought a special item for another user. They have spent vacation time doing home repairs for a fellow user and have gotten together for holiday picnics. Marriage can even be the outcome to an online transaction. Such as the widowed strangers who met when he sold her a paperback book ($7.10 including shipping) about his hobby, miniature cabinets. They exchanged e-mails and then after one intense weekend of 200 e-mails in 48 hours arranged a face-to-face meeting on Valentine's Day in Alabama. (He traveled from Indiana.) eBay was so delighted by the outcome—they were married three months later—that the company flew the couple to California for their honeymoon.

As an example of the hometown flavor, Pierre cites the eBay Cafe, previously called the Bulletin Board. The old name put off community members for whom it sounded too bureaucratic for the friendly chatter that went back and forth about a favorite collectible. They asked for the change and got it. Collectors who share the same object of desire feel free to set up regular meetings to compare notes, as do the Doll Chatters. They set up a weekly meeting, same time, same place (on the Internet).

Jeff, who is now eBay's billionaire vice president of strategic analysis and planning, seconds Pierre's view of the Mount Everest amount of money that has come their way: "Money has never been the driving issue. The success of eBay has long since passed any measure of what I had hoped to achieve financially."

Pierre intuitively knew that eBay would make a great impact on people's lives. This has always been very motivating for us. For example, I keep a picture of one of our eBay users who was a single mother on welfare until she started selling on eBay. Now she supports herself fully on eBay. There are hundreds of stories exactly like hers and so whenever I start to get wrapped up in the financial metrics I always step back and remember the people that we're doing this for. At eBay, this is a motivating factor that goes beyond any financial results. The other good news is that financial success for eBay has also spelled financial success for the people that use our service. We think of our customers as an army of entrepreneurs who are making a living on eBay—small business people, retirees that are supplementing their income and finding new friends, and folks with disabilities who can buy and sell on a level playing field. It's a really incredible situation that certainly keeps us going.

Pierre has kept eBay true to its egalitarian origins. Affordability keeps the door wide open to sellers: 25¢ to list when bidding starts under $10, 50¢ up to $25, $1 up to $50, $2 above $50. When a sale is made, eBay collects 5 percent up to $25, 2.5 percent for the balance up to $1,000, and 1.25 percent for the remaining balance. In a clear sign that power is delivered to the people, eBay sales average $40.

There's also a place for dreamers in eBay lore, such as the $3 pickle jar that sold for $44,100. It really did happen. The jar was bought at a tag sale by a former antique dealer who realized that it was unusual. He figured it was worth $300 or $400. What happened next is like winning the lottery. The jar was turned over to a consignment shop to sell on eBay at $9.99 to start, with a reserve price of $275. By the end of the first day of a week-long auction, the bidding reached $2,500 on the way to its actual, however esoteric, value in the marketplace of collectors. It could only have happened because of Internet visibility via eBay that drew the attention of serious collectors to a rare 11-inch bottle made in Willington, Connecticut, in 1850. The professional bidder, who acted on behalf of a doctor with a major bottle collection, added a footnote on auction fever: "The collector was prepared to go higher."

When the *Wall Street Journal* tracked down Matt Kursh, Pierre's one-time colleague at eShop (an early electronic commerce company), his flashback confirms what Pierre says about himself. After remarking that "if there ever has been an age for accidental fortunes, this is the time," Kursh remembered Pierre as someone who "has always been very serious, very deliberate, and very good at finding the cutting edge. But of all the people at eShop, I never would have said Pierre was the one who would make the most money."

Neither would Pierre, who has described himself as being a "typical nerd or geek" in high school who wrote code and launched from home what he originally called AuctionWeb, using a $30-a-month Internet service provider. The auction was free to one and all. The response was so immediate and so great that Pierre's ISP soon raised his monthly bill to $250. Pierre had to start charging, but, true to his outlook, the price was minimal, 10¢ for listing an item and then a percentage of the final sale price (5 percent to $25, 2.5 percent over $25). The nickels and dimes poured in immediately, adding up to $1,000 the first month, $2,500 the second. From there on, the monthly totals kept on doubling, month after month.

Here was an Internet venture that started in the black and kept going, financed by its community of customers. In the traditional bricks-and-mortar enterprise, customers are added one at a time by spending money on marketing, advertising, and sales as companies pursue customers. The customers find eBay and rush in on a wave of word-of-mouth, the least expensive and most effective advertising. It's contagious, as Pierre discovered.

> *I think people started using eBay because it was interesting, a novelty. They could, in effect, run their own business, get people to bid as prices went up. It was a lot of fun. Very quickly, they realized they were dealing with other people. Relationships were being built up and then a sense of community developed. The network effect came into play. The value of the network, of being part of eBay, increases every time somebody else joins. So it becomes that much more valuable to be part of the network.*
>
> *We faced competition, even in our very early days, from people who were better funded. They've all generally downsized. The reason is quite simple. If you're a buyer or a seller you're looking for the largest marketplace. That's eBay. If you're a seller, you're looking for two things. Do I sell my item? How much do I get for it? You can only maximize those two things by going to the largest marketplace. It's very hard for a new competitor to pull people away from us or to get new people once they know about eBay. In order to get sellers, you must have buyers.*

In the world of auctions, the audience can go onstage, sports fans can join the game, whenever they want. It echoes the cry of the neighborhood basketball court, "I've got game!" Onlookers can join in at any point. (In what other game, is it so easy to change from onlooker to participant and then go home with a prize?) In the eBay community, while half are only buyers, 40 percent are both buyers and sellers, and the remaining 10 percent are strictly sellers. Bidders are in a competition based on desire and they are rooting for the side that counts most—themselves. All through the auction, expectation mixes with uncertainty. At the end, there is only one winner and many also-rans with their what-ifs. Suspense ends in closure, feelings of victory for the successful buyer, pangs of defeat for the unsuccessful bidder. Then it's on to the next auction.

The experiences of eBay buyers and sellers show how easy it is to feel involved and get hooked. Devotees see eBay as being about people as well as things and as a place of pleasant surprises. "All of a sudden, I had this Internet buddy," reported a glass collector about her online friendship with a fellow collector. A seller in Dallas reported that one of the first items he sold on eBay "was an old *Look* magazine—to a guy in Australia." "It's really changed my life," reported a work-at-home mother who was selling as much as $5,000 in collectibles every month.

Trust is supported, maintained, and strengthened by what amounts to self-policing by the participants via feedback that everyone has access to. One antique dealer describes the way a particularly unpleasant, high-handed dealer has changed as an online seller in the face of eBay's full-disclosure feedback mechanism. The dealer is calloused in face-to-face contacts with customers, but when it comes to the Internet visibility of eBay, he is "terrified" of offending online customers.

To illustrate the geography lesson of the Internet, *Time* zeroed in on an antique dealer in Bismarck, North Dakota (population 54,000), who transformed her local business into a global enterprise via eBay auctions. Examples of what audience size did for sales include an art deco ashtray bought for $20, auctioned for $290; a vase bought for $5, sold for $585; an old tractor sold for $2,300 to a priest from New York. Buyers send her checks from as far away as Iceland, Egypt, and China. The dealer compared before-and-after sales: In the best month at her land-based North Dakota stall she sold 15 items; online with eBay she now "can sell 15 items in an hour." Then there's the Alexandria, Virginia, dealer in collectibles whose shop faded into the background after he got on the eBay bandwagon. He added a warehouse to hold his eBay-bound merchandise and a full-time employee to monitor the hundreds of auctions he posts.

What stands out during eBay's explosive growth is Pierre's steadfast decision making and unerring judgment. At decisive points, he has made the appropriate, practical move, starting with the early months of eBay when he reached out for the business know-how he needed. He convinced Jeff Skoll, a Stanford M.B.A. who was on the fast track at Knight-Ridder, to quit his job and come on board. Together they built eBay's staff, ranging from customer-support employees to techies who know how to get the most out of software and hardware. After moving from Pierre's home office to Jeff's living room, they set up shop in an incubator facility run by NASA and rented 1,000-square feet, bought desks with do-it-yourself assembly, and added folding chairs. Pierre's mother provided a big bowl of licorice for meetings at the office. At three o'clock every afternoon, work was interrupted for Nerf soccer games. The corporate culture was summed up by a consultant as "characteristic of the eBay community itself—eclectic, fun, diversified, open, and down-to-earth. . . . There's a strong sense of entrepreneurial spirit that is common in the eBay community as well as in the company."

Working side by side with Pierre, Jeff watched the workings of his mind. "He's a very cerebral guy. His finest attribute is that he's always able to ask the right questions. If there's something he knows nothing about, he manages to come up with the three or four questions that get to the very heart of what he's trying to find out. I've never seen anyone like him in that regard. He's one of the most insightful, complex individuals you'll ever come across. He can take a whole lot of stuff going [on] around him and figure out the right thing to do. When you analyze and reconstruct his logic, it's there. He has this amazing ability to ask the right questions, learn something really fast, and get to the heart of the matter." Pierre's view of his mental process is more down-to-earth.

> *I try to get to the crux of the matter, using a common-sense approach. Oftentimes, an issue seems to be complex if you take into account a lot of extraneous factors. From a commonsense perspective, forgetting about specialized knowledge, it involves asking: How should this thing work? What should the deal look like? What should a particular feature look like? In my world, it has to do with trying to be as close to the user as possible. I try to remind our people when we're working through problems that we're actually customers, too. How would we want things to work? If we're going to be a user, does this make sense?*

As eBay boomed, Pierre faced up to its incredible prospects and went after venture capital, but not for the usual reason. He didn't need the money. He wanted the credibility. So he approached the prestige venture provider, Benchmark Capital, which provided an initial $6.5 million investment in June 1997 (which skyrocketed to $4 billion in value to become the best return on investment in the history of venture capital). The venture money stayed in the bank while eBay harvested the enhanced image that came from attracting the confidence and the funds of savvy investors.

At the time of the Benchmark negotiations, Pierre predicted that eBay would be the company that "put Benchmark on the map." Jeff shrugged off the prediction as wishful thinking. Now he can only say, "Sure enough, Pierre was right." Another prediction that Jeff can't forget concerned Netscape when it dominated the browser market. At Thanksgiving dinner in 1995, Pierre said that in three years Netscape would no longer be an independent company. He and Jeff bet a dollar, even money, on what Jeff regarded as a sure thing. A month before Thanksgiving 1998, Jeff reminded Pierre that he was about to suffer a loss of face as well as one dollar. Not at all: A week before the Thanksgiving deadline AOL announced the purchase of Netscape. To Jeff, it was yet another example of how Pierre manages "to come up with these wacky predictions that are almost always right."

The Benchmark deal provided a bonus by increasing eBay's appeal in recruiting top talent and in creating buzz for an IPO. The major recruiting coup was the hiring of Meg Whitman as CEO, a fast-track executive whose business background was strictly traditional. After a summer experience of selling advertising for her college magazine at Princeton University, she switched from premed to economics. Then it was Harvard Business School and an M.B.A. in 1977. She worked at Procter & Gamble before moving to San Francisco in 1981 with her husband, a neurosurgeon who became a resident at the University of California at San Francisco. She joined the consulting firm of Bain & Company before returning east when her husband became director of the brain tumor program at Massachusetts General Hospital. Her accumulated marketing experience was in mainline traditional companies—Stride-Rite Corporation, Walt Disney, Procter & Gamble. She also had a disappointing two-year stint as CEO at Florists' Transworld Delivery (F.T.D.) before leaving to join Hasbro in 1997.

At that point, she had what eBay needed—marketing and management experience. (*Time* described her as someone who would bring "adult supervision to eBay.") Pierre could be freed to focus on long-term strategy while she handled day-to-day business operations. When eBay came calling, Meg was a marketing executive at Hasbro (whose products include Mr. Potato Head), with a focus on brand building, just what eBay wanted. Benchmark partner Robert Kagle, who was in the middle of the search as a member of eBay's board of directors, spelled out the major job requirement. "I was looking for a brand builder to make eBay a household name. Understanding technology was not the central ingredient. You have to get the emotional component of the customer experience in your gut."

In contrast, Pierre had lived in cyberspace since his high school days. Born in Paris of a French mother and Iranian father, Pierre moved to Maryland as a child when his father, a surgeon, began a medical residence at Johns Hopkins University Medical Center. As a teenager, he kept sneaking out of physical-education classes to play with his high school's computer. This led to his first programming project: to write a program to print catalog cards for the school's library at $6 an hour.

While at Tufts University in Medford, Massachusetts, he wrote a program to help Apple Macintosh programmers manage memory and distributed it online as "shareware." It was not a business success. He asked users to pay on the honor system, but all he received in checks was barely enough to pay for the postal box he rented to receive payments.

After Tufts, his first job was in the software engineering business as a developer of customer applications for Claris, a subsidiary of Apple Computer. In 1991, Pierre became cofounder of Ink Development Corporation where he led an exploration into the then unknown territory of Internet shopping. At the end of 1994 he left the company, which was renamed eShop and subsequently acquired by Microsoft in early 1996. Pierre's next stop, before starting eBay, was at General Magic where he developed a Web application, among other Internet projects. At school, at play, and at work, his was in the world of cyberspace.

Meg, however, as a prototypical product of the world of bricks and mortar, had never even heard of eBay when asked to leave her fast-track position at an established company like Hasbro to head an upstart company nestled in San Jose. On top of that, she was anchored on the East Coast, with two sons settled in school and a surgeon-husband ensconced at Massachusetts General. She turned eBay down, but did make a weekend trip to look the company over. Once there, she discovered a company with a cult following, heard the testimonials of its users, and listened to enthusiastic briefings from venture capitalists. As much as any eBay online visitor who gets hooked, she was converted.

In coming on board in March 1998, she joined millions of eBay converts, half of whom, she reports, find out about the online auction from friends, relatives, or colleagues. Meg the marketer identifies this as the "best kind of advertising" on two dimensions. "It's the lowest cost. In addition, if you told me about eBay and I get on eBay and I can't figure out what to do, I call you."

Meg, who's committed to maintaining eBay's informal culture, has made the adjustment from traditional to Web management. She has spelled out the differences by comparing the "Web way" with the "old way:"

- *Decisions* made in a matter of days or even hours instead of months. Meg's "main advice" to online entrepreneurs is: "Fasten your seat belt. This is a far faster world. You have to be more nimble and far more willing to make decisions without nearly the kind of data and analysis that I used to have at Hasbro, Disney, or P&G."
- *Focus* on selling consumers an experience rather than products.

- *CEO* micromanages the company image rather than monitor it.
- *Management style* is more approachable instead of hands-off.
- *Strategy sessions* might be needed several times a week, not just once or twice a year. "At Hasbro," Meg recalls, "we would set a year-long strategy and then we would simply execute against it. At eBay, we constantly revisit the strategy—and revise the tactics." At eBay, she meets three times a week with her staff to keep up with what other auction sites are doing and to figure out what to do.

She identifies staying close to the customer as a "critical" difference, particularly at eBay, which is in the business of enabling individuals to do business with each other "in a way that's completely new and powerful." As an enabler, eBay brings its users together and then gets out of the way while at the same maintaining a continuous user watch. The feedback is immediate. eBay has tried out thousands of ideas via live discussions and instant surveys (within an hour, 4,000 responses come pouring in). Within 20 minutes after a new feature is added, Meg reports, eBay has "a very good sense of what the adoption rate is going to be." As soon as new products are added, they are monitored and changes are made as soon as possible. "Some of our best ideas—like feedback profiles, which are now central to our service—have come from our community of users."

The feedback forum highlighted by both Pierre and Meg illustrates the democratic style and the openness of eBay. It's essentially a credit-rating system based on the first-hand experiences of the participants. It's like asking customers about their purchases from a used car dealer. Positive or negative, it's powerful testimony that goes beyond kicking the tire and listening to sales talk. Then, for good measure, bidders can contact sellers for answers to questions that concern them. Fans would argue that for smaller transactions, which are the bulk of eBay sales, the feedback forum provides enough protection.

In her CEO role, Meg played a major role in getting the company ready to go public by traveling all over the country to spread the word about eBay. The message was heard. eBay's IPO on September 24, 1998, started at $18 and closed at $47, up 160 percent. That was only for starters. The following May the stock was up 1,019 percent, enriching Meg with her stock options—as well as Pierre and Jeff and all the other employees. For good measure, Meg's executive role won national recognition when both *Money* magazine and *Business Week* named her one of the top 50 CEOs in the country.

Meanwhile, Pierre's sense of social responsibility became increasingly visible as the eBay Foundation that he and Jeff started benefited and boomed. It was established in June 1998 with 107,250 soaring stock shares (which split three to one on March 1, 1999). The Foundation reflects the eBay company culture—"clever, unique, passionate, and eclectic." A month after its founding, Pierre posted a letter to the eBay community explaining the founding premise: "Personally, I have always believed in helping people to become the best they can be." Hence the eBay foundation was set up to support organizations that help people become their best. As to his own fortune, Pierre is conscious of the fact that his "family needs a small fraction of his billions." So he and his wife are focusing not on consumption that makes a statement, but on philanthropy that makes a difference. He's working hard on doing it right.

> *It's very much an accidental fortune. It's not something we went after. For me, and I think for a lot of my peers, it tends to generate a sense of responsibility.*

It's almost as if it's not my money that I can go out and waste. It's something that I have to do good with. So my wife and I are spending a lot of time on our own foundation [separate from the eBay Foundation] trying to figure out what we want to do, what kind of positive social change we can work toward with these resources. It creates a sense of obligation and responsibility to do the right thing. We're really fortunate being in this position. Sure, we work hard, but I think that people are being rewarded these days to a much greater extent than people who worked equally as hard in previous generations. So we have a responsibility to do something good with our resources.

As for eBay, at its multi-billion-dollar heights it has remained what it was at its 10¢ beginning, towering above the online auction world with a two-part siren call to one and all everywhere:

Sell what you want with you're-in-charge selling: List your item for sale, name your minimum bid, decide on the number of days for auctioning it, include a photograph if you want.

Find whatever you want: a mint condition 1954 hula hoop, large Sutsuma vase, 12-piece brass padlock set, African powdered glass beads, folk art cookie press, art deco chrome toaster, Eddy Van Halen's guitar pick, 1940s Mini Craftsman blowtorch, ancient Greek coins.

Buy or Sell or Both. You can have it both ways. All you need to do is sign up with Pierre Omidyar's "efficient market."

For him, high points in eBay's success are letters from customers who report that their lives have changed because his online auction enabled them to turn their hobbies into their businesses. Just the way eBay unexpectedly turned out for Pierre Omidyar. "They became accidental entrepreneurs and found that they could quit their jobs."

Hold on, Pierre adds, when he applies his common-sense approach to what's going to happen in the Internet world. "We're not 10 percent of the way through. We're just beginning to see new models on the Internet. At eBay, we've done something brand-new that could not have been done before the Internet. A lot of other companies are taking old models and applying them online in a more efficient and effective way, but what they're doing is not fundamentally new. So we've yet to see a large number of fundamentally new advances on the Internet."

MARK CUBAN & TODD WAGNER— YAHOO! BROADCAST

"Every Business in the World Is a Potential Customer"

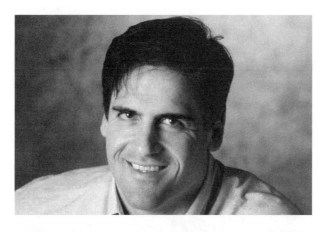

Top, *Mark Cuban;* bottom, *Todd Wagner.*

10

MARK CUBAN & TODD WAGNER— YAHOO! BROADCAST

"Every Business in the World Is a Potential Customer"

In an Internet-absorbed world, what did two Indiana University graduates living in Dallas do when they were homesick for Hoosier basketball games?

Short answer: They turned to the Internet to hear broadcasts of the games.

That was only the beginning. Starting with an outlay of less than $5,000 and in less than five years, they built a $5 billion-plus company. As fast as things happen in the world of Internet entrepreneurs, they don't come faster than the milestones in the meteoric rise of broadcast.com.

> *Summer of 1995*—Mark Cuban, the technological half of the duo, was sitting in his Dallas apartment, having a beer with Todd Wagner, a college friend who had become a high-powered corporate lawyer. Todd was thinking out loud about how it would be cool if they could listen to Indiana games on the Internet in the fall. Todd said to Mark, "You're the geek, you know this Internet stuff. Figure something out."

Same year, September—Mark "figured it out," after investing $2,995 in a Packard Bell 486 PC and about $1,000 for network equipment. Add in $60 per month for an ISDN line and they became Internet broadcasters. An entrepreneurial *aha* was not far behind. "I looked at the Internet and saw the technology for streaming (transmitting audio and video over a data network)," Mark says. "Everyone else was using the Internet for text and graphics, while no one was taking advantage of streaming. Looking at the business applications, I saw them as huge." So with Mark as president and Todd as CEO, they founded AudioNet, starting out with one PC and three employees operating out of Mark's spare room.

July 17, 1998—The company went public at $18 a share as broadcast.com and hit $72 the same day, the kind of stock market run-up that turns Internet entrepreneurs into billionaires. At that date, it was the largest one–day gain in Wall Street history. (At one point, between January 6 and 11, 1999, the stock soared from $81 to $285.)

July 20, 1999—Yahoo! paid $5.7 billion in stock and options to acquire broadcast.com.

Mark uses a muscle-bound metaphor to describe the stakes. "This is cable on steroids. What cable did to TV, the Internet will do to cable. This is not about a 500-channel universe. It's about 5,000 channels, about 50,000 channels. The Internet is an unlimited spectrum." Mark then adds without any hesitation, "I think we have the chance to change the way the world communicates and just make an obscene amount of money along the way. Every business in the world is a potential customer."

As broadcast.com grew, revenues poured in mainly

from advertising at first and then later from business broadcasting—within businesses, business to consumers, business to business. At its core, broadcast.com is a "distributor," as Mark and Todd describe an enterprise built on powerful and deceptively simple projections:

- Content is king, regardless of the medium of transmission, method of distribution, or means of access. Advertisers will pay to reach individuals who are accessing content and businesses will pay to transmit information both internally and externally.
- The Internet is rapidly moving beyond text-based content to audio and video, toward a multimedia spectrum.
- Distribution of content will be in increasingly high demand on the part of businesses around the world and will command a continuously growing audience in the foreseeable future. That makes distribution the crucial enabler.

"We talked to the investment community about how the Internet would evolve into a second generation," Todd says. "We called it the 'second wave' story. The Internet was largely text and was going to become multimedia and nobody else was close to having the amount of content that you could get from our site from a multimedia perspective. We could support the largest audience of people for that content. It was the story we told and a story that got people excited. It was a story of content and distribution combining to raise the barriers to entry."

When broadcast.com was acquired by Yahoo!, nothing changed, except ownership. Todd and Mark continued to run the enterprise, now called Yahoo! Broadcast, as the leading broadcaster of streaming media programming on the Web, able to deliver live and on-demand audio and video programs over intranets as well as the Internet.

Programming comes from 500 radio stations and affiliates and 70 television stations and cable networks. Indiana University's basketball team is now only one among 450 college and professional sports teams on the programming menu. A digital distribution network is transmitting high-speed, high-quality audio and video that virtually any Web delivery mechanism or device can access. And the access is live or on demand.

What does this mean to end users sitting at their PCs?

It means that anywhere in the world and at any time they can log onto broadcast.com to watch their weather forecaster back home predict rain or shine or see and hear their company president outline a new company strategy. They can watch movies, listen to CDs, view TV specials, enjoy the latest episode of their favorite prime time programs, follow the stock market, even tune in on flight control communications from New York's Kennedy Airport. Less than four years after webcasting a local Dallas talk show, broadcast.com drew 1.5 million viewers with an exclusive webcast of Victoria's Secret New York fashion show in February 1999. It was the Internet's biggest live event and a rousing rebuttal to early doubters and their initial putdown, "Why would anyone want to configure a $4,000 computer to make it work like a $6 radio?" Like many other Internet skeptics, they missed the point.

As Todd points out, the meaning of a network is drastically changed in the new mode of thinking that characterizes Internet entrepreneurs.

> *As everything becomes digital, we deliver that digital content over the network, which could be the Internet or other transports as well. That could be a wireless or wired network, it could be via satellites in the sky, via fiber, via cable. You'll then receive it through a whole bunch of different devices. The Internet shouldn't be*

thought of as wires connected to a PC, but rather as a network through which digital content will traverse and be accessed by some device by end users.

As the industry matures, the technology itself will become less important. What will become more important is who has audience and eventually who has brand. And that was a key part of what we were trying to build and certainly a key part of why we did the deal with Yahoo! with its 100 million registered users and more than 120 million unique visitors a month. We felt it was the only company that was Internet-centric, aggressive, and layered perfectly with what we were doing.

What we've done is redefine what a broadcast network means. We know that we can reach more people in the office during the day than traditional media can. We reach more white collar office workers than ABC, NBC, and CBS combined. Why? Few of these people have radios or TVs on their desks. But they all have computers. That, by definition, redefines a network. Personal computers become digital devices for accessing television, radio, and all sorts of business content. As everything becomes digital, you open up a whole new world of possibilities for what you transmit. So we've redefined what a broadcast network is. It's no longer just what you watch at home.

Todd, the accomplished deal maker, characterizes the broadcast.com success story as "15 ducks in a row that lined up every step of the way. . . . If any are missing, you can't connect the dots from the starting point to the $5.7 billion sale to Yahoo!" What he calls the "foundation duck" combined commitment, determination, and sweat equity with the right fit of two Indiana basketball fans as partners. They were propelled by an "absolute won't-lose mentality, sheer tenacity, and work ethic."

The fit could not have been better, as they are the first to affirm. "Todd and I created a great company because he was the exact right partner at the exact right time," Mark says. "My skill set did not include being organized. I was Ready, Fire, Aim. Todd as a lawyer kept our focus on selling and accomplishing things and kept everything running. We complement each other so well. His organizational skills, his ability to analyze things, his ability to negotiate and do deals—I couldn't dream of doing. It just blows me away. He was the "perfect partner." Todd adds: "What Mark and I brought together was unique as a skill set. Between the two of us we could cover almost any topic. Mark is technology and marketing bent, something that is so important in an Internet company, while my bent is toward business and deals, which is very important in a young and growing business. We were able to leverage each other's skills in a way that most companies are not able to do right out of the box. You put those two skill sets together and one and one make five."

As best of friends, they had a running head start as partners, but, as Mark points out, they also had to work at partnering. They learned to deal with their disagreements by respecting each other's areas of expertise and bringing differences of opinion into the open. "We get along great, but we battled along the way. It's natural when you have two successful people who sometimes think they know everything. It's been a wholesome type of relationship where it's been okay to vent at each other. Quickly in the space of four years we got to the point where we respect what each of us does best."

By the time Mark and Todd decided to become business partners, they were well prepared as Internet entrepreneurs, though not as high school or college geeks. In college, each of them took only one computer course, in FORTRAN (which they recall as worthless). "Everything I know in technology," Mark reports, "I taught myself. I have a good aptitude for it and it's a matter of how hard you work at it." Todd points to the "good news" for entrepreneurs: "Technology changes so quickly that it gives everyone the opportunity to get up to speed. It changes so quickly that what you knew two years ago is largely irrelevant. Nothing is set in stone. Opportunity is open to anyone who has the desire and the motivation to dig in and learn, who's willing to spend the late nights and the weekends to get up to speed. That's why I had the chance to do what I did because five years ago there were no Internet experts."

In Mark's case, an entrepreneurial mentality developed early. At 12 years old, he had, of all things, a garbage-bag business. It came about after he asked his father for a new pair of basketball shoes and was told he could save the money from his allowance or earn his own money. When his father asked Friday-night poker friends for suggestions on earning money, they came up with the garbage-bag idea. Mark went from house to house offering to deliver a supply of bags every week. It worked. "No one in his right mind would ever think of a garbage-bag route. Probably no one ever since has. But I made money doing it."

In high school, it was stamps. He became a collector and started visiting stamp shows. On the day he sold a stamp that he had bought for 50¢ for $50, he recognized opportunity. "I realized that not all markets are efficient and not everyone does his homework. I did my homework better than the next guy and saw that I could take advantage of the inefficiencies." In his junior year of college, he took advantage of another "inefficiency." This time it was a chain letter with a $50 price tag. He added a wrinkle by personally collecting the $50. He ended up paying money to himself. In his senior year, he paid his way by investing $2,500 for part ownership in a local bar that was turned into a favorite haunt for students.

After college, he was drawn into the beginnings of the computer industry. At 24, he was selling local area networks and became an early U.S. reseller of Lotus Notes as it became one of the top-selling software packages. He founded MicroSolutions in 1983 and developed it into a leading U.S. systems integration firm. *Inc. Magazine* listed it among the top 500 fastest-growing privately held companies. In 1990, when Mark sold MicroSolutions for $3 million to CompuServe, his company had 85 employees and revenues of $30 million. The sale provided Mark with venture capital of his own. He became president of Radical Computing, a venture capital and investment company specializing in high-tech companies. He also continued to do his homework, taking into account the mistakes repeated from the early days of the PC and software. He reports making "a boatload of money" investing in the stock market. One jackpot move was shorting Netscape.

Meanwhile, Todd was coming from a complementary direction. He was making his name and fortune as a business lawyer at the high-powered Dallas firm of Hopkins & Sutter. A certified public accountant (CPA) as well as a graduate of the University of Virginia Law School, he made partner at the age of 32 and became known as an accomplished deal maker. He found that he felt a camaraderie with the entrepreneurs on the other side of the table, much more than with the lawyers. "I always liked entrepreneurs; they were aggressive and were risk takers." He also had decided that he didn't want to be a lawyer for the rest of his life.

> *I think that so much of success in business and for that matter even in life is pursuing your passion. To me, that's the only way to be successful and I wasn't*

passionate about what I was doing. I wanted to do something that I could be excited about. I really felt that the business world was where my aptitudes were. Besides my legal training, I was a business major in college and also a CPA. I felt these were great springboards that I could leverage if I could get in the right environment. I just had an entrepreneurial bug and was at an age where I was old enough to be taken seriously and still had the energy to go out and do it. I didn't want to wake up 20 years later and say that I wished I had tried something. I saw that the Internet was going to be the next big thing and wanted to get out in front of something as opposed to getting into something after it matured.

When Todd told Mark that he was ready to walk away from a six-figure salary and a law partner's perks to start a business venture, he passed Mark's litmus test for an authentic entrepreneur. "I'm a big believer that the way you test if somebody really believes in a concept is whether or not they quit their jobs and get to work. If Todd hadn't been ready to quit his job, it wouldn't have been the same partnership."

Mark, who was sitting comfortably on a multi-million-dollar portfolio, was originally only going to help out as the "technology geek" for Todd's webcasting enterprise, but then he got "excited" by the prospects and began believing in it to the tune of ultimately investing half his assets. "I didn't look at it as a risk. I told people when we started hiring that if we're in business in five years all of you are going to be millionaires [thanks to stock options]. If we do a great job, the company is going to be worth billions of dollars."

The first test of the concept was further away from the $5 billion outcome than a pickup basketball game in a school yard is from the NBA championship finals. The partners approached the Dallas talk-radio station, KLIF-

AM, and asked if they could broadcast their programs, starting with a local favorite of sports fans, the Norm Hitzges Show. Mark recalls their opening gambit. "We walked into the station and said, 'You know, someday there are going to be radio superstations on the Internet. Let's work together and test it to see if there's really a business here.' " KLIF, which had nothing to lose, said yes.

Mark and Todd started by taping KLIF broadcasts, digitizing the recordings, and posting them on their web site with an invitation to surfers to access them. Mark went on the Internet in pursuit of listeners with no idea of what to expect as a response to his invitation, "Hi, gang, if you're interested in Dallas sports and stuff, come to our web site and tell me what you think." In their exuberant outbursts, Mark and Todd would type, "We are the kings of the Internet. Is anybody listening?" Back came e-mails, some of which replied, "Yeah. Shut up." Soon after, by hooking a $15 radio tuner to the sound card of the computer, they began broadcasting live. Other times they took an audio feed from an event or live program and ran it through a telephone line with an acoustic coupler on the receiving end. The feed would run through the software in the server in a process that would take about eight seconds on the way to providing a live webcast.

They knew they were on the right track when Dallasites from around the world started sending fan letters to KLIF and the AudioNet web site. Dallasites were finding the sound of Norm Hitzges's voice a "cure for homesickness." The responses from office workers alerted Todd and Mark to that "other audience," the booming number of people at work who were attached to PCs as a communications umbilical cord.

On the business side, Todd (drawing on one of his major contributions to the partnership, legal know-how) was busy negotiating deals to webcast programming of stations and sports teams. The teams kept their fans happy and loyal by enabling them to follow the action when they moved away or were traveling. The stations expanded their audiences and boosted the ratings that drive advertising rates and revenues. The stations paid for Internet distribution in cash or provided commercial time, which could be resold or used to promote AudioNet and build audience. Todd was breaking new ground as a first mover in webcast rights. "We licensed a lot of content for multiple years when nobody else cared about it. We were creating something that didn't even exist. Internet broadcast rights—what were those?"

Initially, we just went out and got every and any programming that we could. We'd go to universities and ask if we could broadcast their commencement addresses. We'd ask colleges if we could broadcast their football games. We'd ask radio stations if we could put their signals on the Internet. The idea was to offer as much content as possible—to give people a reason to come to our web site. And you need content that is fresh every day. If you don't get that, you've lost. People will come once and never come back. The game's over.

When I drafted the first contracts and created Internet Broadcasting Rights, there was no such thing. I was drafting rights to distribute content in a wired world and then I'd ask for the wireless spectrum as well. Very early, we were anticipating that the Internet was not always going to stay PC-centric, and it may not always be a wired medium. If another form of distribution were to become more popular, we would have content to make available over that distribution mode as well.

Moving fast, they gained a running head start over potential competition. Plunging headlong into his specialty of deal making, Todd closed some 900 broadcasting deals in the company's first three and a half years—roughly one deal every 36 hours. They had audience and content and were building a network while competitors were struggling to get started. Broadcast.com set up its own private network of satellite feeds and high speed data lines to avoid the crowded Internet. It became a cutting edge provider by having the capacity to multicast to hundreds of thousands of users simultaneously. Todd calls what they did "blocking and tackling."

> *You can talk a big game, talk about strategy and vision, but if you don't do the blocking and tackling every day, you'll never get to the finish line. I think that's what Mark and I were able to do. Blocking and tackling in the Internet world is different from the bricks-and-mortar world. They have to happen in a much quicker way. You still have to act with some precision and you must have a focus on what you're trying to accomplish. But you can't have the many committees and meetings and all the things large organizations have. You've got to trust your instincts a lot. It means licensing content faster and doing more deals faster than anyone else. In our case, by the time that everybody woke up, we already had a huge piece of content share and market share. I focused on getting the deals done and monies raised, Mark focused more than anything on building the network and creating new opportunities. Together we just kept raising the bar.*

"Duck" by "duck," Todd and Mark moved ahead, combining business and technological savvy with the right moves in building, expanding, and establishing broadcast.com as a multi-billion-dollar enterprise with more than 300 employees and 11 offices throughout the United

States and Canada. At company headquarters in Dallas, a converted 50,000-square-foot warehouse functions as one large space that's designed to promote sharing and interaction. The setting is casual, the atmosphere is interactive, the accent is on combining employee exper- tise and enthusiasm. Opportunity seeking is the style Todd and Mark promote. The 100-person sales force, in particular, is empowered and urged to think outside the box in setting up broadcasting and advertising agree- ments that are customized to customer needs. Todd's do- it-now deal-making style is pervasive.

Meanwhile, Todd made sure to protect control of their company by not reaching out for "the most expensive money you ever raise"—initial venture funds that surren- der power to investors. "Our first $2 million came from us, our friends, and 'angel' investors. We retained control of the company and its direction so we could execute on what we saw fit." Then they developed momentum, draw- ing on what Todd describes as their "fire in the belly" and springboarding from one stage to the next.

> We landed a very well-known person in the industry on our board, Mort Meyerson, former president of EDS. That, in turn, helped us get a couple of strategic investors like Motorola and Intel. Then others were willing to jump on the bandwagon. Nobody wants to jump on first. All of a sudden, you've got the attention of the investment banks and you're leveraging their contacts and the dominos begin to fall. First, the regional investment banks show an interest and then the next tier investment banks. As your ducks con- tinue to line up, the big names in the Internet industry, like Morgan Stanley, want to talk to you and take you public. During that process, you've got to be raising money so that you can grow the business and execute on your business plan. In the first year and a half, you

have two full-time jobs, one is raising money and one is executing. One without the other and it's game over.

During all of this, we kept control of the company—the ability to make the key decisions by holding onto the majority of ownership in the company and having majority control of the board of directors. One thing that many entrepreneurs don't realize is how quickly they can find themselves founders, as opposed to CEOs and chairmen. They can wake up one day and somebody tells them, "Uh, guys, you don't get to decide anymore. We're going to bring in a new management team." That happens because of the structure of the system. Having spent eight years doing deals, I knew exactly how the venture capital community works and exactly how preferred stock works. I wanted us to have the ability to make the key decisions. Our attitude was "Who better than us?"

The next phase involves the ducks in the IPO itself and the strategy that you employ for an IPO. Is there momentum in your company? Do you have a strong sales force in place? Do you have a business that scales? Are there barriers to entry? Do you have a way to get yourself to the next level? In going through the IPO process, you want to have analysts that matter on Wall Street covering the company, like Mary Meeker of Morgan Stanley. Her voice is going to get you through the clutter of all the Internet companies and start-ups that are out there. That was another duck in the row.

We had Morgan Stanley handle our IPO, and it was very successful. That was a turning point, as well, because it took us to another level. All of a sudden we went from a company that not many people had heard of to a company that everybody in the business community had heard of. You know you have a successful IPO when it gets you marketing publicity and a lot of momentum—which you must leverage. If you don't leverage it, it won't have done you any good. Now you're on your way and you're in what I call "the gerbil cage," where you must make and exceed your numbers every quarter. You've got to deliver. You're on a treadmill and you can't get off. You have to continue to execute and you have to continue to build the barriers to competition and do all the things that keep you ahead.

In the *first* year of the company, staying ahead meant aggregating content that "plays to people's passions." As spelled out by Mark, that means content that has audience appeal and keeps changing. "We want to aggregate content for which a strong demand exists. And we want content that's replenishable. That's why sports are so important. There's always another game to play, another key play to debate."

In the *second* year, Todd and Mark identified what has become their major revenue producer: business broadcasting. "It was an area where we could control our own destiny," Todd says in describing the revenue shift from 50-50 to 60-40 to 70-30 in favor of business broadcasting revenues over advertising revenues. This encompasses the wide-ranging needs of companies to communicate with customers, vendors, shareholders, and employees. Companies want to broadcast product launches, conference calls, seminars, keynote addresses, distance learning, annual shareholder meetings, quarterly earnings calls, and investor road shows. AudioNet was a first mover, ready and able to provide the distribution. A cross-section of American businesses signed up—Amway, BP Amoco, DaimlerChrysler, Dell, Ford Motor Company, Fox Entertainment, General Motors, Intel, Lucent Technologies, Microsoft, Motorola, Sprint, Texas Instruments, and Texaco.

Further momentum (and revenues) came from Webcasts of live events, more than 36,000 by the end of 1999, that reached both general and niche business audiences. The events ranged from fashion shows to the 1999 Neiman Marcus Christmas Book Launch, from Super Bowls and Stanley Cup Playoffs to John Glenn's historic return to space. What emerged—by design—was a "distribution" enterprise with a discriminating eye and ear, as Todd points out.

> *I think of our core competency as creating things that people can't access anywhere else, creating the right experience for customers, and leveraging that all together so that people don't feel the need to go somewhere else. We become the place where they come to get connected to the multimedia things they care about. If we can do that, then we're doing our job.*

Mark adds his perspective.

> *The Internet is just a transport. We're already using other transports. I don't care if I'm sending over a cellular phone or HDTV [high-definition TV] signals. We use the Internet as just one means of transporting data. It's almost irrelevant which transport we use. We just want to reach the most number of people with the maximum effect. The core competency of the company is distribution. My own core competency is looking at new technology and figuring out the best way for people and businesses to use that technology.*
>
> *I eat, sleep, and read technology. I'll read anything that impacts this business, technical journals, industry magazines. My coffee table is covered with stacks of magazines and books. I spend a good two or three hours reading every day. If I'm at the gym on the bike, I'm reading. If I'm at home in the bathtub, I'm reading. If I'm in bed, I'm reading until I fall asleep. If I'm on an*

airplane, I'm reading. It's absolutely true that knowledge is power.

The biggest limitations of technology are your time and your imagination. I'm looking at technology as an entrepreneur. It's fun to come up with changes when people think this is the way it's always been, and there's no reason to change. Technology is like a ball of thread. It's very, very difficult to get started and to make it into something solid. But once you get going, you can just keep on adding layer after layer. Where most people stop, I look for different combinations in technology that create new and different things. Take the PC monitor. Some people in this industry think it's going to get smarter. I think it's going to get dumber because you can't put new technology in a box that never changes. You want your technology to be where it can change most rapidly. If I were to ask you 20 years ago, "Can you live without a cellular phone?" you'd say, "Sure." Now half, if not most, of corporate Americans can't live without it.

I visualize all the pieces of technology and how they work together and how various combinations make sense. If you're playing an instrument, you understand the changes going from one key to the next and how it impacts the overall sound. You don't think "I'm going to play this note, that note" and so on. You just play it. It's the same way with technology and me. I like to take what is considered conventional wisdom, take different types of technology, and create new opportunities.

While Mark focuses on keeping up with changing technology and its possibilities, Todd keeps up with the business pace of the Internet. His information diet is heavily loaded with trade and business publications (as many as 50) as well as selected online sites. Each from his vantage point carries on a running conversation with the other. Each with a different set of worries, described by Todd.

> *I know Mark worries, among other things, about the proverbial 12-year-old in the garage [coming up with technological breakthroughs] and us being blind-sided. I'm worried about a lack of ability to continue to innovate and execute, about not being aggressive enough, of not continuing to take chances. I look at it as our game to lose and if we lose, shame on us. I look at this as being only the second or third inning of a long nine-inning game. If anybody thinks the game is over, they're kidding themselves. There will be lots more companies that come onto the scene and we've got the chance to be at the big party. But we've still got to execute and we've got to do that every day.*
>
> *In this business, there's not a lot of time for delibera-tions. You must be able and willing to make literally hundreds of decisions every single day. When making those decisions, you've got to be confident that you're making good ones and trust your business instincts, that you're moving the company forward. To me, that is the difference from traditional entrepreneurs. With the Internet, everything's in real time, everything's being compressed. Businesses are made or broken in 12 or 24 months now where it used to be 5 and 10 years. It's a very different process, the stakes are higher and a lot more depends on how you get started.*

Listen to Mark and Todd long enough and the second wave evolves into the third wave, leaving you with the feeling that you are standing on the shore of the future—as wave after wave pounds and changes the shoreline. They visualize the world's largest library where you can access everything anytime thanks to the storage and retrieval power of computers. Not just text, audio, and video, but all varieties of content. Todd points to what will make broadcast.com a winner. Having become part of Yahoo!, the Internet's leading portal for text-based web pages, broadcast.com—as Yahoo! Broadcast—is out to become the unchallenged broadcasting portal, a success defined by Todd.

> *What will make us a winner is a change in people's habits, when their first impulse when they wake up is not to turn on television, but "to turn on this device," which may not look like a PC. When people's first impulse is to go to the Internet for information and entertainment, we win. I think the behavior modification is starting with kids who are 10, 12, 14. Other generations have had the telephone, then the radio, then television; this generation has the Internet. When personalization and customization happen, when everybody gets what they want when they want it via the Internet, we will have won.*

Todd points to opportunities in a world where everything becomes digital. "We can leverage the network, the content, the audience, the brand, because we have an unlimited spectrum. A twenty-first century media company will be a wholly different animal. It will be a world in which you get what you want, when you want it. You'll access it through many devices. A media company isn't going to mean what it used to mean. In a digital world, the challenge will be to serve the audience in a wholly different way."

To which, these first-moving, fast-acting partners add postscripts to identify a defining theme of Internet entrepreneurs:

Todd: "Technology creates uncertainty. It changes the rules. It makes what everyone knew as the answer yesterday no longer the answer. All of a sudden, the experts who had the right answers no longer have them. Technology and uncertainty are creating opportunity."

Mark: "With technology, you can do just about anything."

Photo Credits

Chapter 1   Courtesy of priceline.com.

Chapter 2   Courtesy of VerticalNet.

Chapter 3   Courtesy of pcOrder.

Chapter 4   Courtesy of E*TRADE.

Chapter 5   Photograph by Stuart-Rodgers-LTD. Courtesy of uBid, Inc.

Chapter 6   Photograph by Richard Brown. Courtesy of Go2Net.

Chapter 7   Courtesy of Knight Trading Group.

Chapter 8   Courtesy of PSINet.

Chapter 9   Courtesy of eBay.

Chapter 10   Photographs by Scott Womack. Courtesy of Yahoo! Inc. Used with permission.